# PRAISE FOR
## THE MARTIANS IN YOUR CLASSROOM

"In *The Martians in Your Classroom*, Rachael Mann and Stephen Sandford show us how to build tomorrow's classroom today to prepare our students for whatever lies ahead. Mann and Sandford remind us that, to make our teaching relevant and exciting to students, we 'must address the big issue of exploring and inhabiting the next frontiers of Space. To do so, we have to look up.' When we look up at Space, it's hard not to feel a sense of wonder. With this essential guide, they bring to life Ray Bradbury's dictum: 'It is good to renew one's wonder . . . . Space travel has again made children of us all.'"

**—Talia Milgrom-Elcott,**
executive director and founder, 100Kin10

"Mann and Sandford fuel a twin-turbo rocket onto a different planet regarding their claim about where education was and where it needs to go. Their launchpad reflections offer practical applications and intuitive, orbital expertise that any classroom can adopt. *The Martians in Your Classroom* is not only about STEM, STEAM, or whatever you want to call your own modern version of educating students. It is simply a call to action for new-age thinking, not old-school, status quo instruction. And remember, NASA had to start somewhere too. Grab this book to begin or continue your creative work with kids because they are counting on you!"

**—Rick Jetter, PhD,**
founder of Pushing Boundaries Consulting, LLC,
national education consultant, speaker, and author of six books,
including *Let Them Speak!* and *Escaping the School Leader's Dunk Tank*

"*The Martians in Your Classroom* takes a powerfully unique spin on STEM in our schools and leaves educators feeling inspired and well equipped to toss out the overprescribed and overstandardized learning conditions many of our students endure."

**—Trevor MacKenzie,**
author of *Inquiry Mindset* and *Dive into Inquiry*

D1598625

"*The Martians in Your Classroom* is overflowing with authentic, practical, and engaging ways to empower creative thinking and student voice in the modern classroom. Mann and Sandford have crafted an inspiring read for every educator on the mission to foster student empathy through global communication."

**—Dr. Charlie Miller,**
founder of Flipgrid, professor at the University of Minnesota

"*The Martians in Your Classroom* is not your typical 'how-to-teach' book. Rachael Mann and Stephen Sandford have laid out alternatives to where we need to drive learning and they do so with easy-to-use ideas that will stimulate young minds! Educators will love the ways in which they will be able to incorporate Space and Space exploration into all aspects of their teaching!"

**—Jaime Casap,**
education evangelist at Google

"In *The Martians in Your Classroom*, the authors make a compelling case for more young people to pursue STEM learning. Educators will appreciate this book's readable style and practical suggestions to create the classrooms of the future."

**—Mark C. Perna,**
CEO of TFS and author of *Answering Why*

"Great book! Loved it! Fresh, new, innovative, and just a fun read on a serious topic: our children's education."

**—Dr. Rob Furman,**
principal, author of *The Future Ready Challenge*, #BlogTalkRadio

"*The Martians in Your Classroom* is a compelling narrative that makes the case for STEM and career and technical education by identifying the issues, proposing solutions, and highlighting outstanding program examples. Mann and Sandford help educators, parents, the public, and others better understand how we can empower today's learners for the global challenges that lie ahead."

**—LeAnn Wilson,**
ACTE executive director

"Mann and Sandford marry the passion of teachers with the brilliance of rocket scientists, presenting a compelling case for why we need innovation in our schools. If the first people to walk on Mars (the first generation of Martians) may be in our classrooms today, and if our society on Earth needs a reinvestment in space exploration, what role can the educators of today play in helping students create this future? This book is a launchpad for those who are willing to find out, with pragmatic recommendations for classroom activities, student tools, and deep reflection questions for the reader. Mann and Sandford call for amplifying student voice, globalizing learning spaces, and being active advocates for the future of the human race—in space and at home. This is a book any educator concerned about the future should explore today."

**—Mark Wagner, PhD,**
CEO, EdTechTeam, author of
*More Now: A Message from the Future for the Educators of Today*


"Thinking about 'incorporating Space in every learning space,' as this book invites us to do, is all about inviting wonder into our learning worlds. This book captures the much-needed spirit of invention, creativity, and freedom. Ultimately, as we approach the singularity, the question of whether to approach the design of education in creative ways is not a choice, but an imperative. This book helps to frame considerations about how and why to use STEM and technology in ways that amplify our human presence, connection, and innovation capacities. It's a mandate for modern learning. By sharing strategies that will help educators in our quest to apply immersive technology in meaningful ways, the text includes philosophies that underpin our choices and intentions, as we cobuild more mindful, open learning worlds with our students and communities."

**—Caitlin Krause,**
author of *Mindful by Design*

# THE MARTIANS IN YOUR CLASSROOM

## STEM in Every Learning Space

Rachael Mann and Stephen Sandford

Published by EdTechTeam Press
Cover Design by Genesis Kohler
Editing and Layout by My Writers' Connection

Excerpts from *The Gravity Well: America's Next, Greatest Mission* by Stephen Sandford and Jay Heinrichs (Gavia Books), © Ghaffarian Enterprises, LLC, Reprinted with permission from the authors.

Library of Congress Control Number: 2018942426
Paperback ISBN: 978-1-945167-47-8
eBook ISBN: 978-1-945167-48-5

Irvine, California

# CONTENTS

**1** | Teaching Martians.................................................................1

**2** | We Have Barely Begun ........................................................11

**3** | Forty-Five Years Later ......................................................17

**4** | Saving Humanity..................................................................23

**5** | STEM: Why the Decline Matters ........................................29

**6** | Innovation and Inquiry in the Martian Classroom...............39

**7** | Hubble Huggers Save the Hubble!.......................................47

**8** | Student Voice in the Martian Classroom.............................53

**9** | Globalized Learning Spaces................................................59

**10** | Spinoffs: There's More Space in Your Life Than You Realize! .................67

11 | Rush Hour in Low Earth Orbit .................................................. 73

12 | Aeronautics and the Elusive Flying Car .............................. 79

13 | Off-World Mining........................................................................ 85

14 | You Don't Have to Be an Astronaut to Explore Space! ......... 89

15 | Inspired by Space .................................................................... 97

16 | Space Entrepreneurship...................................................... 103

17 | Red Alert! The Race to Space in Education ......................... 109

What's Next? ................................................................................ 115

Appendix ...................................................................................... 121

Missions for the Martian Classroom ......................................... 133

Acknowledgments........................................................................ 151

Are You Ready to Launch?........................................................... 153

Bibliography ................................................................................. 157

More Books from EdTechTeam Press ........................................ 161

About the Authors........................................................................ 169

Today, your cell phone has more computer power than all of NASA back in 1969, when it placed two astronauts on the moon. Video games, which consume enormous amounts of computer power to simulate 3D situations, use more computer power than mainframe computers of the previous decade. The Sony PlayStation of today, which costs $300, has the power of a military supercomputer of 1997, which cost millions of dollars.

**MICHIO KAKU**

*Physics of the Future:*
*How Science Will Shape Human Destiny and Our*
*Daily Lives by the Year 2100*

# CHAPTER ONE

# Teaching Martians

**W**HEN YOU THINK OF Martians, you may envision the spunky cartoon character named Marvin with beady white eyes, white gloves and shoes, sporting a Christmas costume and a scrub brush on his head. Or maybe an eerie, green being. Perhaps the word brings up images of Matt Damon in the movie *The Martian*, left to fend for himself as he struggled to survive as a sole citizen of the Red Planet. But what about a student in your classroom, a child down the street . . . or in your own home?

The first person to step foot on Mars has already been born and quite possibly is on your class roster! The students in today's schools will not only witness colonies on the moon and Mars, they will explore these new frontiers and pave the way for humanity.

Students in your classroom may sometimes *seem* like alien life forms. In reality, they are experiencing the world—and education—in a way that is so vastly different than what we experienced that it might as well be on a different planet. The way that information is obtained and processed is exponentially different, and the future that we are preparing them for will be even more so.

Learning doesn't happen the way it did in prior decades or even the way it did just a few years ago. Recently, the lyrics to the song "Fire and Rain" by James Taylor came up in a conversation between my mother and me (Rachael). We talked about the meaning of the line, "sweet dreams and flying machines" that we used as a good-night wish growing up. I thought she'd always known the meaning, but she reminded me that in those days she couldn't look up the meaning of lyrics. Real-time information wasn't accessible twenty years ago the way it is today.

In coauthoring this book, not once did I drive to a library to gather resources or open a physical dictionary to look up synonyms or unfamiliar terms. The collaboration took place on shared Google Docs, text messages, and, on occasion, telephone calls—on smartphones. In fact, a large portion of this was "written" with my thumbs. As new ideas came along, I added them to my Google Drive, using my handheld device.

I'm sure we will look back in ten years and reminisce about how advanced we thought our technology was, and how quickly it was replaced with the savvy technology of the future.

## WHAT LED ME HERE: RACHAEL'S STORY

As I think back to my early years as an educator, I remember being introduced to an electronic gradebook as a student teacher and how laborious the technology seemed. My older sister came to visit during this time and showed up with her huge computer and its various pieces and attachments. I remember being mortified as she set it up on the only available surface: the kitchen table. She created an email account for me, and I thought that she was wasting her time and that I would never use it. Staring at a screen waiting for the email to load was painful and time consuming. Little did I know how quickly technology would wrap itself around my world! She asked to see a lesson that I was working on. I gave it to her and moved on to grading papers. Before I knew it, she had turned my boring worksheets into beautiful and impressive documents. Once I started my first year as a full-fledged teacher, my principal assumed that I was tech savvy based on the few exemplars that I used with my middle-school students, so she asked me to teach technology courses the following year. Even after moving into a high-school position teaching career and technical education, I incorporated technology in the classroom and worked to connect science and math content to the skills that would prepare students for their future workplace.

After fourteen years in the classroom teaching subjects ranging from sixth-grade science to technology to culinary arts, I moved on to work at the Arizona Department of Education as the Educators Rising state director. Educators Rising provides a pipeline to ensure a strong workforce of educators for future generations, in particular in the areas of science, technology, engineering, and math (STEM). Through a partnership with the Arizona Science Center, I was introduced to an organization called 100Kin10, which is a network addressing the need for 100,000 new STEM teachers by 2021. In 2016, I was invited to the 100Kin10 Summit in Houston at the Johnson Space Center to work with a group of STEM professionals and educators from across the country to address the projected shortage of STEM teachers over the course of a decade, which in return will continue to result in a shortage of students pursuing STEM careers. In addition to recognizing the magnitude of this problem, we were able to see firsthand the impact that STEM has had on the world around us. We were invited to tour Mission Control Center, where human Space flights were managed. Milt Heflin, retired director of flight control, shared the lessons learned from the Space missions and gave us a tour of the center. I was blown away by the technology that sent man to the moon. From rotary dials to pneumatic tubes, I was fascinated by the idea that this technology enabled us to send humans to the moon and back, and yet we have so much more technology, not only in our classrooms, but in the devices that students carry around in the palms of their hands and the smartwatches on our wrists. I was moved by this experience and began talking about it as part of a keynote address, encouraging teachers and school leaders to think bigger in education and to rethink how we are "doing" education.

In January 2017, on a short flight from my home in Phoenix to Los Angeles, I was disappointed to discover that the flight wasn't Wi-Fi equipped and I hadn't brought reading materials for the trip. I pulled out the Southwest Air magazine from the back of the seat in front of me and flipped through the pages. An image of the surface of Mars with the line, "The red planet is within reach. Now it's time to start thinking even bigger," grabbed my attention, and I began reading the article by Stephen Sandford titled "Beyond Mars." He wrote about the impact of NASA spinoffs on the world around us, projected advances in Space travel, and outlined what we need to do to ensure that we move forward in education. I started following the author on social media and referencing his stats in presentations and workshops. I eventually reached out to him through LinkedIn to see whether he would be available for an interview for an article in *Techniques* magazine. After a few phone conversations and meeting in person while in Washington, DC, to speak at a STEM consortium, we talked about building on the research for his first book, *The Gravity Well*, and coauthoring a book on the topic from an education perspective.

In an interview with CNBC, chief digital officer of Randstad North America, Alan Stukalsky, shared, "There's a lack of education as to what careers are available and what jobs are out there. To get the next generation actively seeking jobs in STEM, they need to be shown interesting, real-world applications, and it starts in schools." This book is an extension of *The Gravity Well*, and our intent is to focus on small, sustainable changes that will have a huge impact on education. We want to blur the lines between content areas and use Space exploration to inspire students to pursue STEM fields.

The United States has a shortage of workers in the areas of STEM. According to research from Randstad North America, in 2016, the United States had three million more STEM jobs than skilled workers to fill the positions. STEM emphasizes the application of knowledge to real-world situations and integrates concepts that are traditionally addressed in separate content areas and classes. Connecting studies to real-life applications in space exploration generates the excitement in the classroom that is needed to make classes more interesting, and the related careers more appealing, and this requires a greater emphasis on career and technology education (CTE) to provide these hands-on opportunities to explore STEM fields.

## HOW IT BEGAN: STEPHEN'S STORY

In my work as an engineer and researcher at NASA, I realized the power of Space to draw students into STEM. Personally, I remember, as a kid, watching the grainy black-and-white images of the rocket launches, hearing the static-filled voice communications between the astronauts and Mission Control, and Neil Armstrong stepping onto the moon's surface. I knew at that moment that this effort was something that I had to join. I later came to believe it must be our collective destiny. I studied engineering and physics, and that dream as a young boy turned into reality. I landed a gig at NASA and spent twenty-eight years as an engineer and mission planner. As the director for Space Technology and Exploration at NASA Langley Research Center, I led teams of engineers, researchers, and mission architects to enable human Space exploration, which led to my current roles working on asteroid utilization, Space policy, and technology transfer to driverless cars.

In my first book, *The Gravity Well*, I address the urgent need for a national Space initiative to create the next economy and ensure the survival of humanity—and of the American dream. To channel the ambitions of our best and brightest youth, I believe we need more than movies about Space. We need a tangible, crucial mission that saves humanity. At any rate, we definitely need more people to go into STEM. America depends on its technological leadership for security and a healthy economy. Yet we are in danger of losing that very technological leadership. I hope this book inspires educators to lead the next generation to dream big and to love math, engineering, science, and technology studies. You and those Martians in your classroom are the only ones who can prevent us from losing our nation's technological leadership.

In education, we must think differently, and think bigger, when it comes to what the next generation must tackle. To ensure the future of humanity and our planet, we must address the big issue of exploring and inhabiting the next frontiers of Space. To do so, we have to look up. We have the technology and ability to have a small colony of humans on the moon by 2030, and the ability to mine ice and precious metals on asteroids by the same date. By 2040, we could have a colony on Mars. By 2050, we could potentially have probes on habitable new worlds. The technology is there, but we need to solve the STEM shortage to make this progress a reality.

---

*You and those Martians in your classroom are the only ones who can prevent us from losing our nation's technological leadership.*

---

The exploration of our Solar System and universe must be an educational imperative. The world still enjoys the educational benefits that came from having a bold Space program in the previous century. Education is about the future, and robust exploration initiatives impact the number of students interested in STEM. Inspiring the next generation through a renewed interest in Space will turn the tide and play a pivotal role in solving the STEM gap.

*The Martians in Your Classroom* isn't a traditional "how-to-teach" book. Alternatives to legacy systems that no longer serve the youth of today will be explored in the next book, while the information found here will lay the groundwork of what led us here in Space exploration and where we need to drive the learning space of the future. This book lays the foundation, while challenging the status quo in education and providing a plethora of resources to support the reader in incorporating Space in every learning space.

---

*"Education is our passport to the future, for tomorrow belongs to the people who prepare for it today."*

—Malcolm X

## WHAT IS A MARTIAN CLASSROOM?

The Martian Classroom is located here on planet Earth and is the learning space you cultivate each day as an educator. It's more than Space; it's the future of education and where we need to drive this learning space to equip the youth of today for what lies before us, both on and off of planet Earth. The Martian Classroom questions legacy thinking and systems that no longer serve the youth of today while driving innovation and bringing a universal perspective to education. The Martian Classroom embraces the concept of "backward design" by looking forward to the forecasted advances in the world around us and asking what skills students will need to succeed in a society that will look vastly different in the coming decades, and designing the learning space and content to prepare students to create this future. The Martian Classroom embodies individualized learning, mastery learning, and most importantly, frustrating learning, as you will discover in the chapters to come.

Space exploration is used in every subject area and grade level of the Martian Classroom to inspire the Martians in your classroom (also referred to as "Gen Mars" throughout the book) to pursue STEM areas and to cultivate that interest. Just as we have inventions that are spinoffs and improve our everyday lives, the science, technology, engineering, and math learned through the study of Space results in spinoffs at the academic level as students learn to think differently and to innovate.

*"The best way to predict the future is to create it."*
—Peter Drucker

## GET READY TO LAUNCH!

At the end of each chapter in this book, you will find a "Launchpad" with activities and prompts. The launchpad is designed to initiate further inquiry, discussions with other educators, and activities in the classroom, and to introduce resources for further exploration.

Do you have other Mission or Launchpad ideas? Share them out with the education community on social media using the hashtag #MartianClassroom.

---

For a helpful listing of
terminology and more resources,
please see the Appendix and visit our website:

# MartianClassroom.org

---

The exploration of space will go ahead, whether we join in it or not, and it is one of the great adventures of all time, and no nation which expects to be the leader of other nations can expect to stay behind in the race for space.

**PRESIDENT JOHN F. KENNEDY**
*speech at Rice University, September 12, 1962*

# CHAPTER TWO

# We Have
# Barely Begun

**W**HEN WE THINK OF the first moon landing, we remember Neil Armstrong taking one long step onto the dusty lunar soil. We remember his words about a "giant leap for mankind." Images of the American flag, the footprints, and maybe Alan Shepard swinging a six iron in the weak gravity come to mind. The other landings, the Space Shuttle, the International Space Station, and the robots sent to distant planets were all impressive feats, but pale in comparison to landing on the moon.

## WHY SPACE?

Some ask, *"Why does Space exploration matter? Aren't we pretty much done in Space? Isn't the Space Race over? We've set foot on the moon, a foreign body in Space. We've sent probes all the way to Pluto and beyond. We've even put robots on Mars. What else could we possibly do?"*

NASA and its partners make daily discoveries about our sun and the Solar System, about the origins of the universe, and about the future of the planet we occupy. What else can be done? The Martians in our classrooms can mine the water that lies beneath the poles of the moon. They can explore lava tubes on Mars that may be warm enough to sustain life—including human life. They can build floating stations in the dense atmosphere of Venus and break through the ice into the liquid ocean of Jupiter's moon Europa. They can see whether Saturn's moon Titan, remarkably similar in size and structure to Earth, is suitable for settlement. The Martians in our classrooms will mine asteroids for precious metals, and reap the immeasurable treasures that arise from the inventions these missions require.

## MOVING IN

In NASA's current work, the agency plays an integral role in upgrading the nation's air-traffic control system, in predicting the weather in Space as well as on Earth, and even in creating the elusive personal air vehicle, the flying car.

So far, we have taken baby steps into Space. We've dipped our toes into the shallow waters of the universe, and the next steps entail moving in. Space travel is more than an act of exploration. It is an act of creation. Invention is the twin of discovery. The intellectual public asset created by the American Space program has a direct impact on the way we should approach education, knowing that for upcoming generations, the ability to access and obtain new information will be more beneficial than rote memorization of facts and figures. The astonishing range of products and innovations that came out of past initiatives is among the most pivotal in the history of humankind, not to mention the benefit of increased international cooperation and the demonstrated value of inspiring young people to go into STEM.

The world respected the United States for exploring Space with courage and foresight. The challenge of the Martian Classroom will help us choose courage once again.

No, we're not finished in Space. We have barely begun. It starts with the leadership in education, to prepare Gen Mars for what lies ahead, and give them the space to create our future.

# LAUNCHPAD

1. How would education be different without the moon landing?

2. What contributions to the intellectual public asset are not directly or indirectly the result of the education system?

3. How do we ensure that as educators, we are leading the changes that need to occur in education to ensure that education is relevant and that we are equipping students for their future reality?

We will return American astronauts to the moon, not only to leave behind footprints and flags, but to build the foundation we need to send Americans to Mars and beyond.

**VICE PRESIDENT MIKE PENCE**

# CHAPTER THREE

# Forty-Five
# Years Later

**A**s of December of 2017, the most recent footsteps on the moon were made forty-five years ago. One of the greatest feats of mankind, and it happened almost half a century ago.

In fewer than four years, NASA achieved six successful lunar landings—the first on July 20, 1969 and the last on December 19, 1972 with the Apollo 17 mission. NASA and the last few Apollo crews made great strides by, among other impressive feats, deploying a lunar rover and exploring the moon for multiple days. But as astronauts geared up for the next stages of exploration, President Richard Nixon placed a capstone on the youthful Apollo program, like the beardless Greek god for which it was named.

Most had believed that the original, "giant leap for mankind" was the first of many. To them, *Star Trek*, which began broadcasting at the same time Apollo was getting off the ground, seemed like a prophecy. Certainly, the world would see weekly flights to the moon by the early seventies, as the German rocket engineer, Dr. Wernher von Braun, had envisioned.

After all, the Wright brothers' first flight was relatively recent history, and people still remembered it had taken a mere eleven years from that first flight at Kitty Hawk to the first commercial plane trip out of St. Petersburg-Tampa. The timespan between the first transcontinental airmail service to the establishment of the first transcontinental airline? Three years. The span between the Soviets' first rocket and the Americans' moon landing? Twelve years. The optimistic anticipated similar strides in the Space industry to accelerate. If Space flight matched that momentum, what would keep us from continuing straight on to the next planet?

## A SHIFT IN PRIORITIES

President Kennedy set Apollo in motion to beat the Russians, and thus the Space program received generous funding. But eventually, the political fuel for Space exploration began to diminish. The historian William Burrows argues that Apollo had been undertaken "for exactly the wrong reason."

Perhaps that is true. On the other hand, maybe it was precisely the right reason for the time. Apollo provided a momentous, peaceful demonstration of American systems at work, to persuade other nations to choose our systems. And maybe that is still a good reason for an ambitious Space program.

The Space Race had also developed an industry which had become economically indispensable and had taken on a momentum of its own. The question was how to keep that momentum going in the most cost-effective way possible. Their decision: a reusable spacecraft which would send people into orbit. And so was born the Space Shuttle.

# REUSABLE SPACECRAFTS AND UNMANNED SPACE PROBES

*Columbia* took off in 1981, completing twenty-eight flights over the next twenty-two years. It, and the four other Shuttles, notched a total of 135 missions, launching satellites and carrying out experiments in Space until the program ended in 2011.

Right at the tail end of Apollo, in 1972, an orbiter called Mariner 9 mapped nearly all of Mars and sent back the first photos of the Martian moons, along with a massive amount of data and tantalizing hints of life. During our nation's Bicentennial, the Viking landers, equipped with a biology instrument to detect life, descended on Mars. They showed solid evidence of water and generated data that took two decades to examine fully.

Meanwhile, other probes were leapfrogging Mars and heading to the outer reaches of the solar system. The Pioneer series set speed records after they launched and sling-shotted past the Red Planet. Pioneer 10 reached the speed of 82,000 miles an hour. In 1973, it brushed by Jupiter, taking pictures just 81,000 miles above its surface. The probe showed that Jupiter's Great Red Spot is probably a gargantuan storm. Pioneer 10 then soared on the solar wind, passed Neptune's orbit, and in 1983 left the solar system, where it continued to send back data.

Pioneer 11 took more pictures of Jupiter, explored Saturn's rings, and examined the planet's moons. The Mariner series took many close looks at Mars. The probes told an alarming story: Venus is far hotter than its position from the Sun would warrant. Consisting almost entirely of carbon dioxide, Venus's atmosphere offered planetary proof of the Greenhouse Effect.

Politics played a huge role then as they do now. At a time when other countries, notably China, are making strides toward sending humans to the moon, the United States has a renewed interest in not only sending astronauts and robots to the moon, but also in creating an outpost on the moon as a staging platform for missions into deep Space.

# LAUNCHPAD

1. How does discovery (the result of exploration and science) contribute to our security and the betterment of life for the Martians in our classrooms?

2. Have students research Jupiter's Great Red Spot. How might understanding this storm enable us to understand Earth's atmosphere better? nasa.gov/feature/goddard/jupiter-s-great-red-spot-a-swirling-mystery

3. What is ticker tape? What are examples of modern day versions of a ticker-tape parade?

4. When do you predict the first astronaut will step foot on Mars?

5. Who is Apollo? Where did other Space programs get their names?

6. Why does planetary proof of the Greenhouse Effect for Venus matter to us here on Earth? In addition to science, how does this discovery connect to other subject areas?

7. Did you know that NASA has thousands of lesson plans and other resources available for use in the classroom? Check out the resources here: nasa.gov/audience/foreducators/index.html

I don't think the human race will survive the next thousand years, unless we spread into space. There are too many accidents that can befall life on a single planet. But I'm an optimist. We will reach out to the stars.

**STEPHEN HAWKING**
*The Daily Telegraph, October 16, 2001*

# CHAPTER FOUR

# Saving Humanity

**W**HEN THE TOPIC OF exploring Mars or discovering inhabitable planets arises, a common assumption is that rather than taking responsibility for the damage that we have done to our own planet, humans will simply hop from planet to planet, using up all the resources. In reality, the more we learn about other planets, the more we appreciate our home here on Earth. The idea of creating colonies on other habitable worlds and mining asteroids is, among many other reasons, to help save our own world. The goal is to ensure the survival of humanity, in the event that a threat of human extinction were to occur.

## DOOMSDAY

Algorithms are pretty good at booking travel, providing friend suggestions, determining what ads should pop up in our feed, and even predicting human reactions. But what about more profound questions, such as the longevity of our species? Researchers from astrophysicists to zoologists use sophisticated computer models to predict the eventual extinction of the human race. Many of these models indicate that our species may survive for another century or two—a thousand years, possibly. Beyond that, however, the outlook seems grim. Name your poison:

- Climate change dries up much of the planet, ruins our food crops, makes the oceans rise, and triggers a refugee crisis and global wars.
- Nuclear war or terrorism causes a breakdown of civilization and mass starvation.
- An epidemic decimates the population before a cure is found.
- An asteroid or comet smashes into the planet, causing a cataclysm of volcanic eruptions, earthquakes, tsunamis, and a pall of ash that destroys almost all vegetation.
- Cosmic rays from a quasar silently kill all living things on Earth.

Most may have forgotten a real-life doomsday scenario that is missing on the list: the hole in the ozone layer. During the 1970s, scientists speculated that chlorofluorocarbons, or CFCs, posed a risk to Earth's atmospheric sunscreen, a layer of oxygen molecules that shield the planet from deadly ultraviolet rays.

Research confirmed that a hole in the layer had opened over Antarctica. NASA sent up satellites during the mid-1980s to measure the extent of the problem. From the vantage point of Space, they proved that the hole not only existed, but it was also expanding rapidly. Eventually, the ozone would disappear altogether. The research was so conclusive that, in 1987, every member of the United Nations signed a protocol to phase out the use of CFCs in aerosol sprays and refrigeration. Scientists now predict that the ozone layer will fully recover by 2070. In short, we are not going to die from hairspray.

But what about the problems that remain? NASA satellites look back at Earth more thoroughly than any other nation's satellites, public or private. We happen to be very good at taking selfies of our own planet. These satellites show the amazingly complex relationships among the atmosphere, the oceans, and land ecosystems—all the systems we have to understand to correct the factors that tend to make our planet habitable to humans.

---

*"The vast loneliness is awe inspiring and it makes you realize just what you have back there on Earth."*

—Jim Lovell

## WHAT DOES THIS MEAN FOR GEN MARS?

Smart, ambitious youth tend to fall into two basic categories: those who want to change the world, and those who want to save it. Either ambition can lead to great progress or blow everything up. To channel the ambitions of our best and brightest youth, we need more than movies about Space. We need a tangible, crucial mission that saves humanity, and this relies on more young people going into STEM.

---

*"As go the schools, so goes the economy. This is our future workforce and these are our future leaders."*

—Ken Scribner
Superintendent, Fort Worth ISD

The United States depends on its technological leadership for security and a healthy economy. Yet we are in danger of losing this advantage. Our university system, as challenging as it is politically and economically these days, continues to be seen as a model by the rest of the world; more than half of students pursuing PhDs in science and tech in this country are from countries outside of the United States, who return to their home countries after graduation. Those lecture halls used to be occupied by mostly Americans. Inspired by the Space program, the number of American math and science PhDs more than tripled during the sixties. After the end of Apollo, that number began to decline, and today there is a severe shortfall. America spends more than $1 trillion a year on education, but it has trouble recruiting its young citizens into STEM. Meanwhile, other nations are doing all they can to invest in education, with the hope of leading the world. This global interest in STEM isn't a bad thing. When we colonize Space, we will not do it alone. To achieve our highest goals in Space requires a human-wide effort. That means cooperation between countries, even rivalrous ones. But if we don't take the lead, who do we want to lead us?

## LEADING THE WAY

To retain our technological leadership, to continue to explore and discover and invent, to lead the world in saving humanity, private industry is building most of the equipment that goes into Space. But the leading-edge research and risk-taking must be spread over our entire society, because no single company in its right mind would subject stockholders to this risk.

To restore faith in ourselves and our future, we have to put ourselves in the shoes of our forefathers, the very first Americans who came to the land bridge that stretched through hostile waters toward an unknown land. They must have held long debates about the risks and rewards of pushing forward. Only those brave souls who took risks eventually saw the rewards.

Are we going to be the generation that paves the way forward in Space exploration?

# LAUNCHPAD

1. Learning about the hole in the ozone layer enabled us to do something about it, thus reversing the damage. How might studying the threat of human extinction and the doomsday scenarios help prevent such a disaster from occurring?

2. What doomsday scenarios are preventable? Guide your Martians in a conversation about sustainability and the benefits of taking care of our planet.

3. Host a *Shark Tank* in which students select a doomsday scenario and come up with potential solutions to prevent or prepare for such a threat.

4. Why does it matter who takes the lead in Space exploration?

5. What are the risks and rewards of a renewed interest in human Space exploration?

With ten of the top fourteen fastest growing industries requiring STEM training, we know the future of our country's workforce depends on STEM education. In order to prepare students for those careers, teachers need to maintain strong connections with STEM industry.

**100KIN10**

# CHAPTER FIVE

## STEM: Why the Decline Matters

**A**CCORDING TO THE WHITE House, only sixteen percent of American high school students are interested in a career in STEM and proficient in math. Lockheed Martin says that "if tech companies don't motivate the next generation now, there simply won't be enough people to fill those jobs and build aircraft and spaceships in 20 years." The Bureau of Labor Statistics (BLS) forecasts that total employment will increase by almost 9.8 million jobs by 2040. The information sector will account for 3 out of 20 of the fastest growing industries, with the "increased need for software to keep up with newer and faster technology" driving the projected employment growth. What does this mean for education?

The obvious response is that we need to rethink graduation requirements and add more technology classes to course offerings. According to a 2016 Gallup study on computer science education, only forty percent of principals in K–12 schools in the United States report having at least one computer science class where students can learn how to code or do computer programming. Although this is up twenty-five percent from 2015, it is not enough to meet projected demands. One of the big issues is a shortage of teachers who are qualified to teach computer science curriculum; sixty-three percent of principals and seventy-four percent of superintendents who do not offer technology classes attribute this lack of qualified teachers as a barrier. We again have the chicken-and-the-egg dilemma: a shortage of STEM teachers to prepare students for these careers. A clue to this shortage could be the fact that a public school teacher makes a median annual salary of $54,980. Compared with a STEM job, a potential pay cut of over $23,000 a year is a hard sell to someone considering a career switch to education. This is where closer ties between education and industry come into play. Business and industry have a vested interest to ensure the next generation of STEM employees. Industries are already partnering with schools in some places to provide an employee to teach related content areas at no cost to the education institution. Exemplars of education and industry partnerships are explored later in this chapter.

While an estimated 1.4 million U.S. science-related jobs will exist by 2020, American college graduates are expected to fill less than a third of them.

One out of twenty students in American colleges is a citizen of another country, yet more than half of all master's degrees and PhDs in STEM subjects go to foreign citizens. Non-Americans earn fifty-seven percent of engineering doctoral degrees, fifty-three percent of computer and information sciences doctoral degrees, fifty percent of mathematics and statistics doctoral degrees, forty-nine percent of engineering-tech and engineering-related doctoral degrees, and forty percent of doctorates in physical sciences and science technologies.

## WHY DO THE STATS MATTER?

Why is this a problem? When we look at the world's most significant challenges, most require solutions related to STEM. Based on this data, only a fraction of our country has the knowledge or skills to solve these issues. If we are to remain relevant and maintain our standing among nations, STEM education must be top of mind for every educator, politician, and citizen. Whether it's discovering the cure for cancer, creating algorithms and systems for transportation, detecting the next terrorist attack, or developing the technology to send humans to Mars, the answer lies in equipping the Martians in our classrooms with the knowledge, the skills, the space to create, and the inspiration to do so.

*The answer lies in equipping the Martians in our classrooms with the knowledge, the skills, the space to create, and the inspiration to do so.*

Kids are natural explorers and problem solvers. Much of what looks like play is where real learning happens. In addition to the lack of STEM educators, we must look at what is happening in the classes as well. A sophomore in high school recently shared with me (Rachael) why she "hates her science class." Each day they watch a video for twenty minutes on VHS, and then the teacher gives them a packet to complete. Once a week they have a quiz. When educators are using the same archaic lesson plans from twenty years ago, it's no wonder the Martians in our classrooms are bored to tears and "unplug" during the school day. But is it really the teachers' fault if they are not given opportunities to leave the classroom in order to learn the cutting-edge technology through conferences and professional learning? The unfortunate truth is, the people who are attending the education conferences are sometimes those who need the new pedagogy and tools the least. Administrators and district personnel flood these events in the name of "trickle down learning." But very little trickles down to those in the classroom—and much is lost in the transmission. Providing educators with opportunities to hone their skills and add new methodology to their practice by attending professional learning workshops and conferences ensures that teachers are abreast of the latest research and delivery models so that students are receiving relevant information and skill sets in a format that is digestible.

## A FASTER WAY FORWARD THROUGH PARTNERSHIPS

Western Maricopa Education Center (West-MEC), located in Arizona, is a model for creating systems to ensure quality instructors with STEM expertise and providing opportunities for these instructors to continually stay abreast of the latest advances in education and in the workplace. West-MEC's tagline, "A Faster Way Forward," defines not only the opportunities that are afforded to students, but how they approach everything they do in education by thinking outside of norms and the status quos that exist in the field and finding innovative solutions and approaches to building a prototype for education.

West-MEC superintendent Greg Donovan and the Director of Business Partnerships, Diane McCarthy, attended a meeting where the needs of the energy industry were discussed. They listened to the concerns around filling the impending vacancies and reached out to industry leaders, letting them know that West-MEC could help to solve this problem. They created a new energy and industrial technology program and a partnership to meet the needs and to give career opportunities for students. Palo Verde Nuclear Generating Facility provided one of their employees, Rickie Timmons, to serve as an industry mentor and classroom teacher for the program while still receiving the same pay grade and benefits through the company. West-MEC provided the training and an instructional coach to assist Mr. Timmons with writing lesson plans, learning how to manage a classroom, and delivery of instruction to ensure that he had the support needed to be successful in this new role.

Partnerships such as this are a win-win for everyone involved. The instructor receives the same compensation while having an opportunity to give back and make an impact through sharing their expertise with students and the fulfillment associated with making an impact on youth in the community. The students receive high-quality instruction that prepares them for the real workplace. The education institution has an industry partner that informs them as to the current needs of the workplace and a STEM expert for students without the additional cost. The industry partner can "grow their own" and ensure a pipeline of talent for the organization, while not limiting student potential.

When asked about the partnership between Palo Verde and West-MEC, Mr. Timmons shared the following:

> Industry needs to be invested in the training of the future workforce. Industry and businesses have more to offer than money or donations of equipment; the people working for companies have a wealth of knowledge in their fields of expertise. Educational institutions need to build a relationship with a variety of industry and business partners and tap into the current workforce to provide the instruction in these fields. This could save educational institutions the expense of hiring these experts and provide companies with another option to be invested in the development of the future workforce. Another untapped source is the near-retired or retired personnel from industry and business fields; companies may choose to extend a near-retired employee's time to provide instruction or retired personnel may be willing to volunteer or work part-time. This provides additional options to companies to be invested in the development of the future workforce and defer the cost away from educational institutions.

> All companies have some form of community relations. The traditional ways of reaching out to communities need to be rethought by both industry and communities. The wealth that companies have to offer is in the form of the people that make up that company and their skills, knowledge, and experience in their chosen fields.

Brady Mitchell is a former instructor in West-MEC's Automotive Technology Program and created a unique partnership with Subaru of America, the retailer. By infusing Subaru's Web-Based Training (WBT) into the existing curriculum, West-MEC has ensured that students have the ability to take most of the entry-level training required for all Subaru-U partner schools and an opportunity to participate in an apprenticeship program. As an industry partner, retailers have the ability to take an active role in their local partner schools in shaping their employees of tomorrow. There is no cost to the student to participate in this program, and students are able to build on and apply Physics, Chemistry, and advanced technology to the work they are doing.

> "This unique partnership between Subaru and West-MEC offers an accelerated pathway for our students. Once the students graduate, they can start working right away at any Subaru dealership at an apprentice level, or continue on to post-secondary to pursue a degree in applied science in automotive. The true benefit is that our students can become a certified Subaru technician almost 2-3 years quicker than someone who pursues a traditional route to certification."
>
> —Brady Mitchell
> West-MEC Curriculum, Assessment,
> and Instruction Specialist

## A FASTER WAY FORWARD THROUGH HUMAN CAPITAL MANAGEMENT

*The most powerful predictor of student achievement is the quality of relationships among the staff.*
—Harvard Principals Center

West-MEC is also an exemplar of human capital management. The organization recognizes and values employees, knowing that they are the most significant asset and the greatest predictor of student success. They provide many avenues of professional growth to ensure that educators are equipped to provide cutting-edge instruction to meet the needs of students. Each employee creates a professional growth plan and self-identifies areas that they would like to improve in or even develop a new skill set. These areas range from learning how to use a new piece of equipment or technology related to their content area to reading a book on how to have difficult conversations and applying this in their work or personal life or signing up for an online course or an in-person class related to the growth area.

In addition to providing staff with access to a team of instructional coaches and professional development staff, and a menu of workshops, online classes and webinars, and one-on-one guidance, employees are invited to participate in the Industry Update Program. Teachers who work in secondary CTE programs have the option of completing a paid externship during a summer, winter, or spring break to update curriculum and teaching methods to meet the ever-changing advances in business and industry. This means that instructors can provide students with relevant, up-to-date information and ensure that they are prepared with the skills needed to succeed in the workforce.

## THE BOTTOM LINE

Until education is elevated as a profession and educators are paid a competitive wage, the cycle of teacher shortages in STEM will continue to create a shortage of STEM offerings, and thus a shortage of students entering STEM professions. In the meantime, exploring innovative solutions and partnerships is crucial to combatting the STEM shortage in education, and thus, in our workforce.

# LAUNCHPAD

1. If selecting just one area to focus on as a nation that will solve the STEM gap, what would it be?

2. The teacher shortage is a national issue, especially in STEM content areas. Many initiatives already exist to address this, yet the problem still exists. What out-of-the-box solutions have been overlooked?

3. We know that many of the problems require solutions related to STEM. What are some of the big problems that will require an answer outside of STEM?

4. In this chapter, we explored how one school district, West-MEC, is breaking the traditional molds of education and creating unconventional solutions. What districts or schools do you know of that are creating new systems that are providing relevant experiences and opportunities for the Martians in our classrooms and our communities?

5. What are some examples of legacy systems in education that you have observed that served a purpose in the past but no longer serve the youth of today? How do we do a better job of identifying these speed bumps in education so that we can transition to a more effective system?

Challenge your students to ask big questions, un-Googleable questions, questions that cannot be answered by looking in the back of the book. Great things will happen.

**TREVOR MACKENZIE**
*The Inquiry Mindset*

# CHAPTER SIX

# Innovation and Inquiry in the Martian Classroom

**I**NNOVATION IS A CRUCIAL component in the Martian Classroom. Teachers serve as facilitators as students discover, predict, invent, and iterate. The lines of subject areas blur as students discover the principles that mesh to form larger concepts. Mastery learning is emphasized, but not at the sacrifice of the freedom to explore new thought processes and the "what ifs," knowing that unsuccessful attempts are part of the learning process, and frequently lead to the next great idea. Students are the architects of their own learning, with the guidance of the educator. Questions lead to innovation.

## A COMPLEX PARTNERSHIP

How did everyday items come about in the first place? Who came up with that all-important dark substance we drink each morning? Or why are tennis balls fuzzy? Did they initially start out that way? Why do forks have four prongs instead of five?

Most tend to think of science as a series of brilliant thoughts punctuated by bolt-out-of-the-blue discoveries. Think Newton under the gravity-compliant apple tree. Or Archimedes plunging into his over-full bathtub. Never mind that someone had to invent that tub in the first place, along with the means of filling it with the water his body displaced.

One of the most important discoveries in the Martian Classroom is that ideas are built on other ideas. Ideas become inventions.

---

### *"What is now proved was once only imagined."*
### —William Blake

---

## MISSION TO PLANET EARTH

What is the mission to planet Earth? Space offers an unparalleled vantage point for viewing Earth. Only by backing away from our planet can we truly see our nebulous life and how closely related we Earthlings are. This perspective is critical to understand enough about Earth to make good decisions on the ground. The Space-based measurements that revolutionized weather predictions are just the tip of the Earth-system-science iceberg. Only from Space can we obtain the global data we need to unravel the mysteries of our home planet.

For example, it was satellite data that discovered the ozone hole in the 1980s. Satellite data is currently showing us how fast the Arctic Sea ice is melting. We monitor pollution globally to improve air quality around our urban areas. And we are developing a better knowledge of how the climate works, thanks to satellite measurements showing how much sunlight penetrates the clouds and hits Earth, and how much heat leaves it. Clouds may hold the clue to how to manage climate change in the coming century.

---

## "Things are only impossible until they're not."
### —Jean-Luc Picard

Mission to Planet Earth is more than a science program; it impacts every learning space. This mission helps to decide how we will live—and what footprint we will leave for future generations. It provides the knowledge we need to make decisions, ranging from international policy to national laws, from state and local planning to business strategies—even our next economy.

## BIG PROBLEMS FOR GEN MARS TO SOLVE

The Sun constitutes the largest atomic physics experiment in the Solar System, with a series of explosions and release of radiation that determines the very existence of life on Earth, and could just as easily destroy it. Every time the Sun burps (a "coronal mass ejection" in scientific terms), it sends out a spray of particles—a deadly rain that scientists call "Space weather." The magnetic field surrounding Earth redirects these charged particles, so they pass by, keeping the killing rain of rays from bathing our planet. The moon lacks this robust magnetic field. As a result, a solar flare could sicken or kill humans on the moon. The solar weather report can constitute a lifesaving prediction, and we can't make further advances in Space without it. What are other lifesaving protections against a solar flare?

The Solar System operates as a vast climate experiment, and a story whose moral applies directly to Earthlings—and Martians in training. NASA's Planetary Science Directorate sends up probes and robots to our neighbors, retrieving data that reveal the life history of planets. We discovered, for example, that Venus used to be a pleasant, watery, habitable planet much like ours. Gradually, the Venusian atmosphere became increasingly acidic, with more carbon dioxide. The $CO_2$ trapped the Sun's rays, causing the planet to warm dramatically. The Martian atmosphere also used to be much more like Earth's. Mars, too, built up its $CO_2$ levels. What caused the rise in the Greenhouse Effect? Finding out could help us discover solutions for our own planet. Our use of fossil fuels is accelerating the process that took our neighbors millions of years.

**Credit: NASA**

Anyone wondering what Space exploration has to do with Earth science would do well to take another look at the classic photo, "Earthrise," showing our planet from Space and letting us step back from Earth and see it as a whole, in all its complexity. Our studies of the planets in our Solar System could help pave the way to escape Earth, if necessary, or diversify our inhabited real estate.

These are just a few examples of big problems that Gen Mars will be tasked with solving. Challenge students by giving them assignments that do not have an answer key, questions that still do not have answers. When we only teach things that we know the answer to, we are not preparing students to solve the unknowns that the future holds. Give students the ability to search for answers instead of just expecting them to know answers. Changing how we define success in the classroom means getting past the letter-grade system that doesn't prepare students to solve the big, unanswered problems of the world, such as these.

# LAUNCHPAD

1. Think of an item you have used today. What's its history? Where did it come from, and what problem does it solve? Will it continue to solve that problem? Are there other ways to solve the same problem or ways to improve the item?

2. Check out Trevor MacKenzie's books, *Dive into Inquiry* and *Inquiry Mindset*. How might cultivating an inquiry mindset help the Martians in your classroom solve big problems?

3. What other problems still need to be solved?

4. Innovation takes on many forms in the classroom. What does innovation look like in your context?

5. "Only by backing away from our planet can we truly see." Think about this concept in relation to our education system. What are we too close to that is preventing us from making needed breakthroughs in education? What can we do to step back and get a fresh perspective?

6. Along the same lines, Wayne Dyer is credited with saying, "When we change the way we look at things, the things we look at change." How does looking at the landscape of the future workplace through the lenses of Gen Mars change the way we "do" education?

7. What are the issues that we have been wrestling with for over a decade without making progress? How might asking different questions and reframing the problem lead to a breakthrough?

8. Our education system is tied closely to industry; first to agriculture, then to manufacturing, now to technology, and in the future, Space. We have hardly scratched the surface in keeping up with technology. What steps do we need to make in order to ensure that Gen Mars is prepared for future horizons, on and off our planet?

9. In today's education realm, leaders must stay relevant and ensure that they are anticipating needs and potential threats, and search for innovative approaches to learning. What questions should leaders consistently ask? How do leaders best model an inquiry mindset in order to make this process visible?

Don't underestimate the power of your vision to change the world. Whether that world is your office, your community, an industry or a global movement, you need to have a core belief that what you contribute can fundamentally change the paradigm or way of thinking about problems.

**LEROY HOOD**

# CHAPTER SEVEN

# Hubble Huggers Save the Hubble!

**A**STROPHYSICS SEEKS TO EXPLORE everything from the outer fringes of the universe to the beginning of time, all while searching for Earth-like planets. The best-known program in this branch is the Hubble Telescope, with its eight-foot mirror and instruments measuring visible, infrared, and ultraviolet light. Operating in low Earth orbit about 350 miles above the distorting atmosphere, Hubble has produced more data and photographs (not to mention images of gas clouds and star clusters that could be classified as art) than the telescope's creators could have imagined. Scientists have even used its observations to measure the universe's rate of expansion.

## THE OUTCRY

Eventually, Hubble came to the end of its productive life, and its control systems began to fail. To fix the problems and extend the telescope's lifespan would mean risking the lives of astronauts. The 2003 disaster with the *Columbia* Space Shuttle, in which all seven crew members died on re-entry, led to the decision to shut Hubble down rather than take a chance.

And then came a huge outcry, not just among scientists but from the general public. NASA Chief Sean O'Keefe began receiving 400 emails a day from "Hubble Huggers." *ABC News* reported that "thousands" of schoolchildren wrote letters. Senator Barbara Mikulski led the opposition in Congress, and Representative Mark Udall introduced legislation requiring an independent panel of experts to look into the matter. The National Academy of Sciences piled on with criticism of the decision, leading to the resignation of an important NASA administrator.

The agency soon relented and in 2009 sent up a crew to repair the equipment and replace its systems, including a UV instrument thirty-five times more sensitive than its predecessor. The astronauts completed the job in two spacewalks, and to this day Hubble is going strong. Some experts think the telescope could be bringing back images of deep Space into 2030 and beyond. The telescope's fan base also remains strong; its Facebook page has more than two million likes, and more than 1.5 million are following it on Instagram. Saving Hubble illustrates the power of student voice and the collective voice of a society. Thousands of students wrote letters, and these letters made an impact. Politicians, scientists, nonprofit organizations, and the general public came together in volume not only to take a stand for Hubble, but to take a stand for the impact of NASA and the work that put the Hubble Telescope into orbit in the first place.

## THE WEBB

The Hubble is a tough act to follow, but the James Webb Space Telescope, due to launch in May 2020, will seek to outdo its predecessor. Parked at Lagrangian point Sun-Earth L2, it will have some impressive equipment onboard, including a twenty-one-foot mirror and unparalleled resolution, allowing a visual glimpse of the first stars in the universe as well as star-forming clusters. The Webb, in short, will show us our own beginnings. Imagine a video camera that allows us to witness the signing of the Declaration of Independence or Caesar's assassination—only we're talking about the beginning of time itself.

Now imagine being on one of the dozens of teams assigned to this task. They began work in 1996, collaborating with scientists, engineers, administrators, and diplomats from seventeen countries. The plan was to launch in 2011, but cost overruns and technical problems kept setting the date back. After NASA spent $3 billion on the project, the House of Representatives voted to shut Webb down. But the Senate brought it back to life.

This funding story is one that permeates all of NASA's programs. Teams of rocket scientists work with passion on projects that go just so far before wobbling perilously on the vagaries of Congressional budgets. In this case, there is hope that the Webb will end up in Space, parked a million miles from Earth and rewriting the history of the universe. According to NASA, the Webb is scheduled to launch in May 2020. We'll never want to shut it down.

## HOW CAN WE APPLY THIS IN THE MARTIAN CLASSROOM?

There are many lessons to be gleaned from Saving Hubble and the James Webb Telescope. When we believe in something, we have to go after it, even if it means risking failure. Many of the projects that the rocket scientists at NASA pursue are passion projects that may or may not get off the ground. Having a willingness to go after something and put in the hard work, regardless of the guarantee of success or acceptance of the idea is part of the process. What may look like failure at first could lead to future success. For most, the biggest regrets are the things they didn't attempt to do because they were afraid of failure. Elon Musk says it well: "If something's important enough, you should try. Even if the probable outcome is failure."

Having an idea or project shot down feels like a failure, whether it's through the House of Representatives in the case of the Webb, or a *Shark Tank* class project, or not winning first place in a robotics competitive event. Learning to deal with perceived failures is part of being successful in life. Sometimes this means not letting the failure cause you to entirely throw out the idea. Remind students that it takes multiple iterations to get it right. The first draft is rarely the final draft, and what may seem like a failure at first might just be the beginning.

For example, when is the last time you've heard anything about Google Glass? A few short years ago, we thought this product would revolutionize the world around us with a new form of wearable technologies. The hype was short lived, and it disappeared quietly, with the website shutting down in 2015. A 2.0 version on the market now, called Glass Enterprise Edition, is an augmented reality tool designed as a wearable device for hands-on workers in fields such as healthcare, manufacturing, or field services. The repurposed version has received positive feedback so far. According to a review by Europe PMC, "There are promising feasibility and usability data of using Google Glass in surgical settings with particular benefits for surgical education and training. Despite existing technical limitations, Google Glass was generally well received and several studies in surgical settings acknowledged its potential for training, consultation, patient monitoring, and audiovisual recording."

Teaching the Martians in our classrooms to stand up for what they believe in and to use their voices, even in the form of letters, is another lesson from these telescopes, and it teaches agency and advocacy. The youth of today will be sharing and defending their thoughts and ideas with a global audience, which will be explored in the next chapter. It's important to train them to do so in a positive and powerful way.

# LAUNCHPAD

1. Speaking truth to power means standing up for what is right, even if it means risking ridicule. What role do we play in empowering students to make a stand? How do we equip them to do so in a responsible way?

2. Note the critical role of astronauts and robots working together for the biggest bang for the buck in repairing Hubble. Predict what this may look like in ten years as Artificial Intelligence takes on a more significant role in technology advances.

3. Teamwork is key not only at NASA, but in the Martian Classroom as our world becomes more collaborative. What are some potential passion projects for your students as they prepare to create the future of our world?

4. What additional lessons can be gleaned from the Hubble and the Webb?

5. What is too important not to try, even if you risk failure?

If you can't communicate and talk to other people and get across your ideas, you're giving up your potential.

**WARREN BUFFETT**

# CHAPTER EIGHT

# Student Voice in the Martian Classroom

**T**HE ART OF RHETORIC is considered by many to be a lost art. In many schools, presentation literacy is equated with giving public speaking assignments rather than deliberately preparing to effectively deliver a talk. In the Martian Classroom, students learn to communicate and use their voice to make an impact, both in person and virtually, to share ideas globally. The leaders in a Martian Classroom know that it is irresponsible to give a public speaking assignment without first creating a safe environment for students to share ideas, discussing how to calm the nerves, channeling fear into creative energy, and going over all of the "what ifs" that can cause a student to have a dreadful experience in front of a crowd—in addition to creating great content that makes the audience want to hear more.

## FEAR VERSUS DANGER

In his TED Talk, "What I Learned from Going Blind in Space," Canadian astronaut Chris Hadfield shares his experience of learning how to deal with fear versus danger. He explains that preparing for every worst-case scenario prior to going into Space enabled him to calmly work through temporary blindness while in Space while on his first spacewalk. He compares this experience to how we view any perceived danger, such as a fear of spiders, and how to think through the real risks to change how you perceive a situation.

This is the type of conversation that can not only change a Martian's view of public speaking, but turn a terrifying experience into an exciting opportunity. When students are able to conquer this fear at a young age, they are able to communicate ideas that can change the world around them and communicate these ideas in a powerful way.

## JFK RALLIES A NATION

The ideas that have changed the course of history would have never made it off the ground if not communicated in a way that garnered interest and the support of others. John F. Kennedy rallied a nation through his skillful ability to communicate the lunar plan, not only to Congress, but to future generations who still look back at his timeless speech for inspiration.

Selling the plan to Congress and the American people required a feat of rhetoric that matched the cause. Remarkably, Kennedy turned the occasion, at the height of the Cold War, into an argument for peace. Instead of beating the Russians with weapons, America would turn an enemy into a rival. We would vault past the Russians and go all the way to the moon. Kennedy pivoted with remarkable speed; he pitched his argument to Congress just five months after taking office.

Then, in September 1962, he gave his famous moon speech at Rice University. The school had helped arrange the donation of land near Houston, Texas, to establish a Space center, a generous nod to Kennedy's vice president—a Texan. Addressing a crowd of 35,000 in the

Rice football stadium, Kennedy picked up on Eisenhower's vision of a peaceful Space, a frontier, as Kennedy put it, that "can be explored and mastered without feeding the fires of war."

Kennedy's rhetoric worked with Congress, which had a Democratic majority and members eager to see Space facilities and laboratories built in their districts. But the argument never entirely won over the American people. A majority of Americans thought we were spending too much money on Space. At the height of the attempt to send men to the moon— when NASA sent three humans 25,000 miles an hour into Space, circled the moon, and brought them back safely—most citizens opposed the program. Even when, on July 20, 1969, Neil Armstrong and Buzz Aldrin walked on the surface of the moon, almost half of Americans thought the money should have been spent elsewhere. The moral is clear: ideas shape the world around us when communicated in an impactful way.

# LAUNCHPAD

1. Gen Mars holds the next JFKs of this world. The Martians in your classroom may be the ones to change the course of history with the power of their voice. How does this change the way that you view your students, collectively and as individuals?

2. How can you ensure that presentation literacy isn't replaced with simply giving public-speaking assignments?

3. Share Chris Hadfield's TED Talk with your students and use this as a springboard to discuss fear versus danger, and to discuss the worst-case scenarios of public speaking. This will help students to approach the stage with the confidence and help them to get back in front of an audience again, even if they did fumble over a few words the last time they shared their ideas in public.

4. What does the word "rhetoric" mean? What impact did John F. Kennedy's rhetoric have on the Space mission?

5. Read *Thank You for Arguing* by Jay Heinrichs as a springboard for rhetoric in the classroom. Visit his "Argue Lab" for a free teacher's guide, videos on rhetoric, teaching tips, and more: arguelab.com

6. The mission to the moon was opposed by many. It takes guts to stand up against popular opinion and act on a bigger idea. What are some examples of when this has happened in history or your own experiences?

Teachers are no longer the gatekeepers of education. With ubiquitous information available from Google searches, YouTube videos and social media, how do educators navigate the new landscape? It's time to ditch that textbook, engaging students in digital spaces and rethinking our "textbook" beliefs about education.

**MATT MILLER**
*author of Ditch That Textbook*

# CHAPTER NINE

## Globalized Learning Spaces

**Y**OUR STUDENTS MAY VERY well be the first to return to the lunar surface, or to be a part of the first colonies on the Red Planet. But the Martian Classroom isn't just about Space, it's also a metaphor for the future of education and where we need to drive the *learning space* for this future. How do we prepare Gen Mars for a world that will continue to change exponentially?

To start, we need to loosen the ties between education and geography, and this needs to happen now. Expanding the classroom to collaborate with classes on the other side of the globe will prepare them for a world that connects work to global talent.

A globalized workforce is becoming the norm as industries are no longer limited to local talent in a city or community. The Institute for the

Future (IFTF) provides practical insight for organizations to prepare for the world as it undergoes rapid changes. IFTF predicts that our society will move toward a "gig" concept, in which industries find the best talent on a global level for a particular task, rather than relying on full-time employees who punch the clock each day. This change will create a more connected *and* more competitive environment for the Martians in our classrooms, and it is something we can already see.

I (Rachael) recently copresented with an educational leader from Switzerland at The Future of Education Technology Conference in Orlando. We collaborated from the comfort of our living rooms miles away from each other via Google Meet, shared Docs, and Google Slides for months prior to the event without even meeting in person until a couple of hours before our session. The future is already here, and globalization will continue to become a more integral part of our lives and those of the Gen Mars in our classrooms.

Kids get this; they have friends they have never met, but that they interact with on a daily basis. That's already here. We not only need to keep up with the forecasted changes from the perspective of the workplace, we need to keep up with the Martians in our classrooms as well by bridging the gap between geography and education in our learning spaces.

Moving in this direction can be a really good thing. The more globalized we become, the more cooperative we will be. Just as the International Space Station and the first step on the lunar surface were victories for all mankind, global efforts will promote peaceful interactions between nations. Businesses and industries that are no longer tied to local talent will create a more competitive environment for the Martians in our classrooms, and this is actually good news. Here are some reasons why:

- A competitive environment not only ensures the right fit for the gig, it also brings out the best in each of us, as status quo is not an option.
- The Martians in our learning spaces will develop a global language and professional communication skills free of

acronyms, jargon, or regional references. We will be able to solve problems without language barriers.

- We will be able to capitalize on the work of others, rather than duplicating efforts across the globe.

- With a global workforce, cooperation and collaboration will be a must, whether it's within business and industry, the political realm, or advanced missions to outer Space. Efforts such as going to Mars will be an international effort, and will truly be the next leap for humankind, bringing nations together on a common venture, thus promoting peaceful interactions.

What does this mean for educators? Globalized learning spaces are a must. Fortunately, we already have some tools to make this a reality, and additional platforms will continue to be developed. Here are just a handful of tools for global communication and collaboration:

## FLIPGRID GLOBAL GRID CONNECTION
blog.flipgrid.com/news/2017/2/23/global-connections-and-other-fun-things

Digital pen pals, asynchronous video communication, worldwide collaboration—what's not to like about Flipgrid Global Grid Connections? If you have not set up an account already, this is a must-have tool for presentation literacy.

## TED-ED CLUBS
ed.ted.com/clubs

Join students around the globe with TED-Ed Clubs. TED Talks are created for a global audience, and TED-Ed Clubs connect students to the ideas of youth worldwide. TED-Ed Clubs organize "Connect Weeks" throughout the year for students to meet each other on video calls, talk about their cultures, ask questions, and build relationships. Twice a year, TED-Ed Clubs invite Clubs from around the world for TED-Ed Weekend events to amplify student voices from the TED stage.

## MYSTERY SKYPE
education.microsoft.com/skype-in-the-classroom/mystery-skype

Join the global game with Mystery Skype. This tool helps teachers expand their curricula beyond their classrooms to international learning spaces. Two classrooms are matched and they must then guess the location of their Skype partner by asking questions. Students learn about the geography, customs, and culture, and see how similar students are internationally, while learning about what makes each of us unique. Skype has a database of teachers and classrooms looking to connect for this and any other projects.

## HOWJSAY
howjsay.com

Simple words (or complex ones) sometimes trip up even the most seasoned speakers and make it difficult to regain composure. Howjsay is an app that can be used to check the pronunciation of trouble words prior to speaking, identify multiple dialects if available, and translate and pronounce words in different languages.

## VIDEO TELEPROMPTER LITE
videoteleprompter.com

With this free app, students are able to record themselves speaking while reading the words on the screen. This gives them an opportunity to reflect on their own skills as they self-evaluate facial expressions, the tone and pitch of their voice, or the pace of speech. The fight-or-flight response that is activated when speaking in public, or anticipating that others will see a video, causes a natural reaction of speaking at a faster rate. With Video Teleprompter Lite, students can practice slowing down the rate of their speech by changing the speed of the script feed. This is not only useful for improving presentation skills, it's an excellent tool for students who are looking to gain confidence for video conferencing.

# GOOGLE HANGOUTS MEET
## gsuite.google.com/learning-center/products/meet/get-started

With global communication and the tech tools we have at our fingertips, teachers do not have to be the only experts in the classroom. Invite guest speakers from other areas of the country, or world, into your learning space. A few months ago, I (Rachael) was invited to speak to a class of students in Guam, over 6,000 miles away. But with Google Hangouts Meet, we were able to spend an hour together from my living room. Our Hangout was scheduled for 8 p.m. on a Wednesday evening in Mountain Time, which is 1 p.m. on Thursday in Guam (Chamorro Standard Time). The students immediately greeted me by saying, "Welcome to the future!" and referred to me as "the time traveler" throughout the call. How cool is that!

Students have a megaphone in the palms of their hands that can reach the entire globe—and this technology has huge implications. We can help our Martians use it as a force for good and collaboration.

# LAUNCHPAD

1. Pair students up with partners from a classroom in another part of the world. Have them complete a project together using collaborative tools such as G Suite. Concerned about what the answer key will look like? Take this assignment a step further and have students collaborate to solve a problem that doesn't have a solution yet. If they fail, that's okay. The learning that will occur through this creative, collaborative process will be more beneficial to their future than any textbook lesson could aspire to accomplish.

2. This chapter lists a few examples of why global workplaces and learning spaces will be beneficial. What are some additional benefits to education? Drawbacks? Share your thoughts on social media #MartianClassroom to keep the conversation going.

3. Download "The Educator's Guide to Flipgrid" by Sean Fahey and Karly Moura for a step-by-step guide to using Flipgrid and ideas for global connections: goo.gl/CDH8U3

4. As an educator, connect with someone in a similar content area, but on another part of the globe, to plan a lesson or presentation. Have the topic be related to Space exploration in your particular context. How did this compare to similar in-person, collaborative activities?

5. Invite a guest speaker to talk to your class or staff using a video-conference tool. Reflect on the level of engagement and connection of using a virtual tool versus in-person communications.

Innovation doesn't necessarily entail creating something new. It's not the same as invention. Rather, innovation usually involves a fresh perspective on something that already exists—taking an idea, a technology, or a material (or aggregating several) and then considering how their use can create a positive impact in a new and better way.

**SARAH KRASLEY**

*The 6 Questions That Led to New Innovations*

# CHAPTER TEN

# Spinoffs: There's More Space in Your Life Than You Realize!

**W**HEN MOST PEOPLE THINK of spinoffs, they likely think of video games, fiction novels, products, or TV shows like *Young Sheldon*—a spinoff of *The Big Bang Theory*. These are opportunities to dive into a particular character or scene. But what about NASA spinoffs—not the rocket boosters spinning back to earth, but products benefiting humanity, which began as a NASA technology?

Spinoffs aren't just a bonus of the Space program; they're a critical part of the work itself. NASA's annual report, *Spinoff*, credits Robert Zubrin, the legendary founder of Pioneer Astronautics and Pioneer Energy, for leading the invention of technologies that convert the Martian atmosphere into water, oxygen, and fuel. Because the air on Mars comprises ninety-six percent carbon dioxide, Zubrin has pioneered ways to convert gases into useful substances.

For example, he initially speculated that hydrogen could be brought from Earth and combined with Martian $CO_2$ to make methane and water. Besides providing liquid to drink, they could electrolyze the water to produce oxygen for breathing. The excess oxygen, combined with methane, can make rocket fuel to power the astronauts' flight back home. Now that water has been discovered on Mars, hydrogen can be produced on the planet's surface and combined with $CO_2$ to make methane. While inventing the technology that helps make Martian missions possible, Zubin's companies have spun off inventions that produce gas for research balloons. His work with gases may also lead to technology that efficiently extracts hydrogen from water on Earth, providing carbon-free energy.

## SPINOFFS AND THE INVENTION-DISCOVERY CYCLE

The most impactful spinoffs contribute to the invention-discovery cycle, even while boosting the economy. A perfect example is a work contracted by NASA's Glenn Research Center with MicroLink Devices, Inc. Future Space exploration missions may depend on massive solar arrays to provide limitless energy. Illinois-based MicroLink has developed flexible cells that can be mass-produced at a fraction of the cost of existing technology. Besides offering promise for Space missions, the military has been using the cells for power supplies and to power drones. Could the technology exist without the Space program? Yes, probably. But NASA provides an accelerant and a proven mission-driven invention machine. The Glenn contract changes the uncertainty of solar technology into a reasonable business risk for MicroLink. In return, NASA speeds up the invention of massive solar wings that can send instruments and humans to Mars and beyond.

The spinoffs that don't directly go back into the Space invention-discovery cycle nonetheless play a prominent role in the economy, and in improving our well-being. Not all of them have to do with inventions you can hold in your hand. NASA was a pioneer in the development of systems science—the development of methods to manage enormously complex operations. The education community looks to medicine as a model for systems thinking. However, the medical community credits engineers and aerospace for these concepts, and for the application of model-based systems engineering tools to clinical medicine. A new field emerged from this work called healthcare systems engineering, which applies systems engineering tools and systems theory to healthcare delivery.

The code written for NASA, in turn, has formed a rich ore of data that companies have mined in unrelated sectors. For example, NASA's Ames Research Center provided software that allows other kinds of systems to detect problems. CEMSol LLC, a Phoenix-based company that creates healthcare software, licensed system-monitoring software from Ames that uses data to track components of healthcare systems, establish a baseline for normal behavior, and watch for any deviations. The software was designed to warn airline pilots and mechanics of possible impending aircraft failures. CEMSol's Integrated System Health Management programs have been used in medical centers around the world.

## ENGINEERS ARE SPINOFFS TOO!

Among the "spinoffs" from NASA are its engineers, who go on to found private companies. Alliance Spacesystems is one of them. In creating robotic arms for the Mars rovers, Spirit and Opportunity, the former NASA engineers wanted to make it easier to collaborate with computer-aided design documents. They came up with a PDF collaboration code—and spun off another company, Bluebeam Software, Inc., to market it. Bluebeam recently sold to a German tech company for $100 million. How does the software add to the invention-discovery cycle? Engineers throughout NASA, and everywhere else for that matter, now have a relatively inexpensive, efficient way to exchange and mark up PDF design documents, making invention that much easier.

Similarly, back in the Eighties, NASA software engineer Craig Collier wrote software at the Langley Research Center to help design a hypersonic Space plane. While the plane itself never got off the ground, the software did, through the private Collier Research Corporation. Collier perfected his code, called HyperSizer, which allows engineers to model weight and load requirements for various vehicle designs. Recently, the company expanded from commercial aircraft design to optimizing wind turbines.

While many spinoffs continue with NASA engineers founding their own lucrative companies, some of the most significant side benefits of the Space program work in the opposite direction. NASA contracts with private companies to invent solutions to aerospace problems; the companies in turn figure out other, profitable ways to use their inventions. The Goddard Space Flight Center had one such problem when it came time to repair the Hubble Space Telescope in 1993. Hubble launched in 1990 at the cost of $2.5 billion, and astronomers had high hopes for unprecedented images of deep Space. But when the telescope deployed, they discovered to their dismay that a construction error had left the mirror slightly misshapen, rendering the images distorted and blurry. NASA needed a precise way to detect defects so that properly measured replacement parts could fix the scope. Goddard sent out a call to optics companies, and Massachusetts-based AOA Xinetics won the bid with a detection tool. Xinetics, now owned by aerospace giant Northrop Grumman, went on to create a commercial 3D imaging detection device bought by FedEx, UPS, and just about every other major package shipper.

Space exploration aims at the boundaries of knowledge, not just minor consumer improvements. The inventions that arise from the Space program, even those that find use in unrelated sectors, are no accidents; they're integral to the government's mission.

What if we changed the words "Space exploration" to "education" and made this our battle cry? "Education aims at the boundaries of knowledge, not just minor improvements."

# LAUNCHPAD

1. You don't have to go to Space to find NASA technology. Whether invisible braces, infrared thermometers, improved mine safety, or freeze-dried food, Space spinoffs have changed the way we live. If you know someone with a pacemaker, it likely uses NASA technology to keep the body from rejecting it. Visit spinoff.nasa.gov and see if there is a spinoff related to your content area or the grade level that you teach.

2. Set aside a time for students to explore NASA Spinoff and find a technology or product related to a career field of interest. How does, or could, this spinoff add value to the industry?

3. What invention would students want to pioneer if they were to live in a colony on Mars or the moon? Ask them to research whether it has already been invented or whether it is currently being explored.

4. Set aside time for students to explore careers that have been impacted by the technology developed by NASA. Use this as an opportunity to help students develop skills and effectively share ideas as they share their research either in the class or through a video app, such as Flipgrid or Recap.

The wonder is, not that the field of stars is so vast, but that man has measured it.

**ANATOLE FRANCE**
*The Garden of Epicurus, 1894*

# CHAPTER ELEVEN

# Rush Hour in Low Earth Orbit

I**T REALLY WASN'T THAT** long ago when the two greatest superpowers were vying to put satellites into Space. Now, fifty nations have satellites in low Earth orbit. The Martians in your classroom may someday be competing with other industries in low Earth orbit or relying on the technology for other industries.

An organization interested in putting a satellite into geostationary orbit for television broadcasting or military communications from Thailand can have it in orbit 25,000 miles above Earth within two years. What's more, competitors are pushing that lead time down to eighteen months or less. The cost is plummeting, all thanks to competition in private industry.

Already the slots in geostationary orbit and low Earth orbit are beginning to get crowded. At last count, 1,469 satellites were in orbit, a third of them American. Currently, competition exists largely because of governments, and the large price of putting a satellite into orbit—at least $50 million and as much as half a billion. The majority of that price comes from the cost of the rocket, vehicle, and fuel. Most of the rocket, in fact, is fuel—including the fuel required to carry the fuel.

## LOWERING THE COST

To launch a satellite into low Earth orbit, the rocket must push against gravity and atmosphere to achieve a speed of 17,000 miles an hour. For geostationary orbit, the required speed is 6,875 miles an hour. The greater the weight of the launch vehicle, spacecraft, and satellite, the higher the cost. Not long ago, the price per pound of sending an object into low Earth orbit was about $5,000. Now, the Russian Proton-M rocket may have cut that cost by half.

Musk's SpaceX intends to drive the price down still further—far enough to create a true private market in Space. One big cost-saving measure is the reusable vertical takeoff and landing (VTOL) rocket. Both SpaceX and Blue Origin have built working VTOL rockets. SpaceX, with its big Falcon Heavy rocket, promises a price per pound in low Earth orbit of $709. Regardless of whether or not Musk can achieve that goal, the goal itself is crucial. Private industry is exceptionally good at producing technology that can conduct repeated tasks at a low cost. This sort of feat is the basis for whole economies.

Capitalism itself is based on competition, and the number of companies vying to put satellites into Space is growing. Jeff Bezos is one of Musk's most celebrated competitors. But Blue Origin is just one of at least sixteen companies, along with three commercial wings of national Space agencies, making rockets to launch satellites commercially. Two are European partnerships, several American, three Russian, along with Japanese, Iranian, Indian, and assorted multinational firms. All are vying to bring launch costs down.

Another way to lower the cost of satellites is to make them smaller—much smaller. The miniaturization of electronic circuits has allowed for satellites to shrink dramatically. Sputnik, two feet in diameter, could do nothing more than emit radio pulses. The largest satellite currently in Space, a top-secret spy satellite launched by the U.S. military in 2010, is floating in geosynchronous orbit over the equator. It required a massive lift by a Delta IV Heavy rocket, capable of 1.9 million pounds of thrust. While the Pentagon will not release the figures, the cost was certainly substantial.

## NEW MARKETS

By contrast, a new market is springing up for nanosatellites, complex equipment weighing just two to twenty-two pounds. These satellites can be launched individually or in clusters, saving huge amounts of fuel and allowing the development of small, specialized rockets to carry them. Then there are the emerging picosatellites, super lightweights of a couple pounds or less, which can be launched in swarms. Among the most famous is the CubeSat, originally conceived by engineers at California Polytechnic State University and Stanford in 1999. This cube of circuitry and communications equipment, weighing two pounds, can be built and launched for as little as $150,000. A CubeSat can piggyback with larger equipment on a rocket launch, be sent out from the International Space Station, or be deployed in groups to communicate with a mother satellite. CubeSats are ideal for high-risk laboratory experiments—science with a relatively low chance of success. NASA recently announced a Cube Quest Challenge to design picosatellites to orbit the moon in 2018. Five teams, a mixture of universities and private companies, have won $20,000 prizes for completing the first round and will have the opportunity to win. NASA is offering a total of $5 million to teams that meet the challenge objectives.

The Space mission provides a powerful avenue to inspire the bright young minds in our classrooms into STEM, to explore and settle the terrain of Space in our neighborhood of the Solar System. Today we are well on the way toward a developed economy in low Earth orbit. Farther out, Space missions can deliver outposts at the Lagrangian points, the moon, Mars, and asteroids, all within the next generation of students. A full effort will guarantee a dramatic uptick in the number of Martians in math, engineering, science, and technology. And it will nurture highly paid workers who will drive our economy well into the future. In short, the drawing power of Space must be utilized strategically.

# LAUNCHPAD

1. The "Three Satellites Problem" reinforces math in Space while allowing students to solve problems with real-world applications: mathopenref.com/problemsatellites.html.

2. Visit the Physics Classroom for Mathematics of Satellite Motion, Orbital Speed Equations, The Acceleration Equation, Practice Questions, and more: physicsclassroom.com/class/circles/Lesson-4/Mathematics-of-Satellite-Motion.

3. NASA has a slew of rocket resources and activities to incorporate in the classroom. Visit go.nasa.gov/2IgLOIr and add the "A" to STEM for some STEAMY activities.

4. Capitalism is based on competition. Create a project for students to create their own industry for low Earth orbit, around industries such as satellites, tourism, or travel. Create a *Shark Tank* concept for students to pitch their ideas, and then create a business plan and design for their new venture.

5. NASA for Educators has a "Build It Yourself: Satellite!" game on its website for grades five through twelve. Students choose what science they want the satellite to study, such as black holes, exoplanets, star formations, galaxies, or early universes. They then select wavelengths (ultraviolet, optical, X-ray, infrared, microwave, or gamma ray), instruments such as X-ray spectrometer or X-ray camera, and optics such as segmented or single primary. After exploring, students discover which NASA mission has data similar to the mission they have created.

6. Visit the NASA Milestones: Calendar Years 2016–2021 and discover what's next for low Earth orbit, satellites, and more.

In times of change the learners
shall inherit the earth while
the learned find themselves
beautifully equipped to
deal with a world that no
longer exists.

**ERIC HOFFER**

# CHAPTER TWELVE

# Aeronautics and the Elusive Flying Car

*T*HE *JETSONS* **DEBUTED IN** 1962 and depicted what many thought our present day would look like. Now that the future is here, it is not at all what was envisioned—much more advanced in some ways, yet without the strides expected in other areas.

We tend to think of NASA as a Space agency, period. But that first "A" for "aeronautics" in the acronym says a lot about the agency's evolution. Its predecessor, the National Advisory Committee for Aeronautics (NACA), invented superchargers for high-altitude bombers, pioneered wing design during World War II, and provided critical research into breaking the sound barrier. President Eisenhower replaced NACA with the National Aeronautics and Space Administration (NASA) in 1958, as part of an effort to launch a satellite into Space. Aeronautics remains deep in the agency's DNA, and it accounts for an essential set of programs.

Aeronautics is the science and technology of atmospheric flight—in short, anything made by humans to fly, from wings to propulsion to the forces that make the combination take to the air. Aviation contributes $1.5 trillion—more than five percent—to the national economy, and it's one of the few American industries with a positive balance of trade, with a million manufacturing jobs.

Besides providing the brains behind flight, NASA's aeronautics programs work to keep commercial flights running safely with minimal delays. The challenge is to reform the nation's air-traffic control system—a network that uses radar technology developed early in the last century—and add satellite navigation. Besides helping coordinate planes in the sky, the new system will allow the more efficient use of runways and airports, a win for both passengers and our carbon footprint. NASA is also developing next-level technology to automate flight, through the development of what engineers call "autonomous cyber-physical systems"—in other words, flying vehicles controlled by computers.

One outcome of this work: the autonomous flying car. Thank you, Jetsons. You may have seen some of the new flying cars—personal air vehicles, or PAVs—on the Internet. Equipped with folding wings, they can drive on the highway and then, controlled by a licensed pilot, take off from any standard runway.

## WHERE ARE THE FLYING CARS?

There are two reasons why we have not seen flying cars in our early-adopter neighbor's driveway: licenses and runways. The current flying cars are really just highway-enabled airplanes. To make a true flying car requires vertical takeoff and landing, or VTOL. Instead of runways with a minimum length of 1,700 feet, you could have designated parking areas barely larger than the car itself. This would eliminate the runway challenge. Then there's the license challenge; it takes skill and training to fly a small plane, and even greater skill to pilot a VTOL vehicle.

The answer is to create a self-driving vertical takeoff car—a Google car of the skies. This flying car will use a combination of laser sensors, cameras, and satellite-based GPS to detect its location and avoid obstacles. Powerful computer calculations will help it anticipate and avoid bad weather or human error.

NASA has been working on the autonomous component of the PAV, and the technology is advancing rapidly—possibly faster than the vertical challenge. Getting a vehicle to take off and land vertically, safely, with efficient use of fuel, under a variety of weather conditions, in crowded cities or suburbs—ideally without deafening the neighbors—presents a big challenge. But it's conceivable that the first street-legal and sky-legal PAVs could be on the market by 2025.

## UBER

Elon Musk, who, ironically, sent a Tesla hurling through Space on February 7, 2018, noted some challenges with flying vehicles during an interview with Chris Anderson at the April 2017 TED Talk event:

> I'm in favor of flying things. Obviously, I do rockets, so I like things that fly. This is not some inherent bias against flying things, but there is a challenge with flying cars in that they'll be quite noisy, the wind force generated will be very high. Let's just say that if something's flying over your head, a whole bunch of flying cars going all over the place, that is not an anxiety-reducing situation. You don't think to yourself, Well, I feel better about today. You're thinking, Did they service their hubcap, or is it going to come off and guillotine me? Things like that.

Despite the challenges of flying cars, Uber is making headway in putting them on the market. Uber is making a concerted effort to capitalize on airspace as a means to alleviate congested highways on the ground. They have pinpointed 2023 as a projected year for the first VTOLs to be introduced to larger cities, and they will use rooftops for landing and takeoff.

Our economy flows through efficient, low-cost transportation. At the same time, we must reduce our use of fossil fuels if we want to limit climate change. NASA's aeronautics technology can serve as the key to this effort by developing cleaner, safer, more efficient aircraft. The next generation air-traffic control system is well within reach of near-term deployment. The FAA and NASA will have to work together with industry representatives, and research and contract funds need to be freed up to bring the system online.

The flying autonomous aircraft—the equivalent of the self-driving car, will be something that Gen Mars not only witnesses, but will help to spearhead its evolution. Personal air vehicles, perhaps powered by electric batteries, can help relieve our overcrowded airports, save land, and minimize emissions.

# LAUNCHPAD

1. In Tim Urban's entertaining take on the history of the Space Race, he makes this profound statement: "1972 people would be blown away by our smartphones and our Internet, but they'd be just as shocked that we gave up on pushing our boundaries in space." Why do you think we gave up? What do you think we will accomplish in the next year? Ten years? Fifty years?

2. How quickly will early adopters jump on board with purchasing PAVs? What advantages will this provide for our current systems of travel?

3. What changes will Gen Mars see in current and future careers in transportation with the addition of flying cars?

4. Ask the Martians in your classroom to write/speak/draw/animate what they envision for our world in fifty years.

5. Math is a fundamental tool for all engineering fields, in particular, aeronautical engineering. Visit the Khan Academy for personalized learning resources for all ages: khanacademy.org

If you're offered a seat on a rocket ship, don't ask what seat! Just get on.

**SHERYL SANDBERG**

# CHAPTER THIRTEEN

# Off-World Mining

**T**HE WORDS "MINING ASTEROIDS" might bring to mind an image of Bruce Willis sacrificing his life to save Grace and the rest of humanity. In the 1998 movie *Armageddon*, an asteroid the size of Texas threatens to collide with Earth in less than a month, so NASA recruits a team of deep-sea oil drillers to save the planet.

Although the movie is science fiction, someday, perhaps thirty years from now, companies will be mining asteroids. Asteroids contain the same valuable minerals, from gold to platinum, from cobalt to indium, which Space showered upon Earth billions of years ago. One sizable asteroid can hold $20 trillion worth of minerals. On a smaller, more practical scale, Peter Diamandis estimates that a single hundred-foot asteroid can contain as much as $50 billion of platinum. The good news is, we can exploit asteroids without damaging Earth's environment, and the supply is almost endless. The bad news: Asteroid mining will be enormously risky and expensive, at least in the beginning.

The first step is to gain the wealth of knowledge from studying the makeup of the asteroids. The leading program, OSIRIS-Rex, a science-driven mission, launched on September 8, 2016. It is traveling 300,000 miles to asteroid Bennu and will bring back two kilograms (a little more than four pounds) for study. It will arrive at Bennu around August 2018 and will be the first United States mission to return an asteroid sample. This exploration is estimated to cost $800 million, with the rocket itself adding almost $200,000 to the estimated cost. This is being funded by society as a whole: through our government, and in the long-term, high-risk ventures like this with incalculable payoffs are the work of a great nation. The Martians in our classrooms are the future voters and potentially, politicians who will drive future efforts to move us forward to the frontiers that are on the horizon.

Asteroids like this contain more than precious metals; they also contain water and organics that could someday be used as fuel for both robotic and manned spacecraft as we explore the universe. They also provide clues to questions such as where did we come from and what is our destiny as they reveal the history of the bodies that they once composed. Examining the leftover debris helps us understand the formation process of our solar system.

# LAUNCHPAD

1. What additional advantages do you foresee when it comes to off-world mining?

2. What do you feel the greatest concerns should be?

3. What career paths would play a part in such an endeavor, both on and off Earth?

4. Divide the Martians in your classroom into two teams to research and debate why we should or shouldn't move forward in efforts to mine asteroids.

Space is for everybody. It's
not just for a few people in
science or math, or for a select
group of astronauts. That's our
new frontier out there, and it's
everybody's business to know
about space.

**CHRISTA MCAULIFFE**
*teacher and Challenger astronaut*

# CHAPTER FOURTEEN

# You Don't Have to Be an Astronaut to Explore Space!

**N**ASA **IS NOT JUST** astronauts. Nor does it exist only for the physical exploration of Space. America's Space agency isn't even just about Space. Its major initiatives comprise astrophysics (the purest science of the cosmos), the study of our Solar System; aeronautics (focusing on improvements to aviation technology), Earth science, the examination of the Sun, Space technology (which finds new ways to conduct robotic and human missions), and the human exploration program.

## INVENTION AND DISCOVERY

The vast majority of NASA's explorers are not astronauts. A current NASA mission is to create a terrain map of Space—not of planetary bodies, but of the clashing forces between them. But how is mapmaking a kind of exploration? Isn't it merely a precursor? An essential concept of the ancient Greeks and Romans is helpful here. They used this concept to develop two of the most powerful, creative civilizations in human history.

The word for this concept is *inventio*. It means both "invention" and "discovery." The ancients believed the two are inseparable. Nothing gets created wholly anew; it was an ancient Greek who wrote, "There is nothing new under the Sun." Invention meant discovering the available means to solve a problem or do something new.

Engineers understand this concept implicitly. The team that invented the iPhone did not invent the digital music player, or GPS, or email, or the web browser, or radio communication. They discovered a new purpose for each and married them into an intuitive machine for Apple's smartphone. Of course, a great deal of technical wizardry was required to make all these existing inventions play nice together; but the result was pure *inventio*: invention and discovery in one creative act.

*Inventio* is the perfect description of NASA as well. It invents to discover, and the inventions themselves are an act of discovery. While most NASA engineers wince when called "rocket scientists," in a way the label is appropriate. The agency comprises deeply practical people with a passion for discovery. They invent by discovering and discover through invention.

## THE SPACE LANDSCAPE

Back to the mapmaking. NASA assigned me (Stephen) and a group of colleagues the task of determining where to park a new outpost in Space, one that would provide a waypoint between Earth and the moon—an essential step to colonizing both the moon and Mars. This, again, constituted an exercise in *inventio*.

The theory behind Lagrangian points has been around since the mid-1700s, when they were conceived by an ingenious mathematician named Joseph-Louis Lagrange. Born in Italy, he moved to Berlin to become the director of mathematics at the prestigious Prussian Academy of Sciences. He ended up in revolutionary France, where he became instrumental in the development of the metric system. Lagrange helped invent probability theory and advanced number theory. He corrected Newton's theory of sound and pioneered the study of work efficiency, and his calculus equations led to the greatest advances in physics in the nineteenth century. Napoleon, a huge fan (the feeling was not mutual), appointed Lagrange to the position of senator. Engineers revere him for the math he brought to celestial mechanics.

In 1764, using a set of differential equations to calculate the gravitational dance of the Sun, Earth, and moon, Lagrange explained why the moon has one side always turned away from us. Eight years later, he helped solve one of the great mysteries of outer Space: the "general three-body problem." Take Earth, moon, and Sun. You know the initial position, the mass, and the velocity of each. You know Newton's laws of motion and universal gravitation. Now explain how all these forces act upon each other. Lagrange's formulas helped form the math that determined the Apollo flights to the moon. But not until the 1980s did NASA begin exploring the deeper possibilities of Lagrange's math. Then the agency's scientists and engineers started imagining the forces of mass, inertia, and gravity as a *terrain*. And terrains can be mapped.

Figuring out which point in the Space landscape was ideal for the new station involved choosing between two good choices, coming up with a plan to get the station there safely, park it in exactly the right spot without wasting fuel, and help create a railroad grade through Space. Easy peasy, right?

Take a look at this from the most straightforward Lagrangian terms. The Apollo program was the equivalent of the Lewis and Clark Expedition, a set of explorers who took the straightest possible path (as much as any path that involves multiple orbits around planetary bodies can be straight), over hills and mountains, using whatever energy it took to go from point A to point B. The astronauts went to the moon, taking everything they needed with them, and then they returned home, all in about a week. This, on the other hand, involved dealing with the problem of shuttling equipment, supplies, and teams of people back and forth, not once but many times. Following the same path as Apollo would require enormous expenditures of fuel. It would be like trying to build a railroad simply by following Lewis and Clark, with cliffs and canyons along the way. Instead, the best grade would be a "flat" course with the most neutral gravitational forces, which meant going a much longer distance to avoid the rough places.

L1, located closer to Earth than the moon, was too easy. Getting there meant barely leaving our terrestrial neighborhood. L2, on the other hand, presented a challenge. It lies closer to the moon than to Earth, and it would stretch NASA's technological prowess to the fullest.

After weeks of hashing out ideas with some of the most brilliant minds on the planet, the result was a detailed plan consisting of designs, analyses, drawings, trajectories, and cost estimates to park a Space station at L2 with a direct view of deep Space and the far side of the moon.

Seven months later, NASA scrapped the mission concept. Agency leaders chose not to send a station to L2. Instead, NASA would focus on an entirely different task: to land a robot on an asteroid and bring back a sample. The engineers and scientists that I worked with on this mission were understandably disappointed, yet the work was not in vain.

Without leaping into Space, each of us had explored it—with math, powerful computers, and a whiteboard. The calculations and plans can also be used to get to the asteroid—and to Mars for that matter—and they will help catalyze other missions.

## CARTOGRAPHY IN EARLIER DAYS

Christopher Columbus's mission to the New World was an act of cartography; his initial assignment by the king and queen of Spain was to map a course from Europe to Asia. Getting to China wasn't really the point; not to mention the fact that there happened to be a continent in the way. The point of Columbus's mission was a map, one that later voyagers could follow. The team at NASA did the cartography in front of a whiteboard and in the computers of our teams around the country.

You don't see this sort of work in the news media, understandably. Just about every week the news bears the latest successful NASA missions, complete with colorful photos. Meanwhile, some of the best minds in the agency are working on tools and methods that never get off the ground—at least in ways the teams intend. No private company would put up with this kind of research and development of apparent dead-ending. Spread out over a hundred million taxpayers, however, the risk becomes positively palatable. And ultimately it produces benefits for the greater good.

## DEAD ENDS

The missions may never leave the ground, but they live on as acts of invention and discovery. The tools and methods get used by other missions and worked into ever more sophisticated tools and methods. The labors on L2 will be incorporated into the asteroid landing and other missions. Multiply this effect among the many significant programs at NASA, and the dozens of current missions, and the vast creative engine of *inventio* thunders.

There's just one devastating problem: The asteroid mission has not received the go-ahead, either. The dead ends keep multiplying. Still, teams continue to work on missions that may or may not get off the ground, creating a vast wealth of data and technology across all branches of NASA and beyond.

# LAUNCHPAD

1. Have you ever thought of "cartography" as a Space mission? Visit "Careers at NASA" to discover other surprising career opportunities.

2. Learn more about the elusive "dark side" of the moon: pbs.org/newshour/science/never-see-far-side-moon

3. Some of the best tools at NASA never get off the ground, yet the research and knowledge that increases from such attempts create a wealth of data and technology. What would this look like in schools? How do we create a learning space designed to encourage innovation?

4. View John Green's TED Talk, "The Nerd's Guide to Learning Everything Online" for an interesting perspective on cartography.

We should try to leave the world a better place than when we entered it. As individuals, we can make a difference, whether it is to probe the secrets of Nature, to clean up the environment and work for peace and social justice, or to nurture the inquisitive, vibrant spirit of the young by being a mentor and a guide.

**MICHIO KAKU**

# CHAPTER FIFTEEN

# Inspired by Space

**S**PACE ENTREPRENEURS OF THIS century all have one important thing in common. More than having the smarts for science or the desire to be rich and famous, what really inspired these individuals is that, as children, they were enthralled by America's accomplishments in Space. For example, Elon Musk, founder of Tesla and SpaceX, believes in the Space program as a source of inspiration as he, too, was pulled into Space by Apollo.

Burt Rutan, one of the first private Space pioneers, followed a similar trajectory. An aeronautical engineer by training, he started out as a civilian employed by the Air Force before founding his own aircraft company in 1974, which specialized in homemade airplane kits. He went on to pursue loftier goals, eventually winning the Ansari X Prize by sending the first private rocket to carry two people 100 kilometers above Earth twice within two weeks.

Isaac Newton's famous expression, "If I have seen further it is by standing on the shoulders of giants," rings true in aerospace as well. Rutan was building on previous discoveries—including the NASA rockets that preceded SpaceShipOne. The SpaceX Prize was backed by an insurance company, with the $2 million premium paid by Anousheh Ansari, an Iranian immigrant and telecom entrepreneur, along with her brother-in-law. But the idea for the prize came from Space entrepreneur, Peter Diamandis, founder of a company that makes microsatellites. His inspiration for the prize came from the $25,000 Orteig Prize offered for the first successful transatlantic flight in the early 1900s.

Charles Lindbergh is credited for his contributions and work to usher in the age of commercial aerospace. Taking on the challenge of wealthy hotel owner Raymond Orteig, Lindbergh was determined to be the pilot to make the first solo transatlantic flight without making any stops. In 1927, Lindbergh flew 3,600 miles from New York to Paris in under thirty-five hours, and won the Orteig Prize.

When Lindbergh, nicknamed "Lucky Lindy," won the Orteig, he became a global celebrity. There was talk about him running for president. His achievements inspired thousands of young men and women to go into aviation. One aerospace historian wrote recently, "The prize spawned the $250 billion aviation industry."

Private Space exploration has a lot going for it, not least the unflagging enthusiasm of its technology-born champions, who are themselves inspiring young people. While they vary in age—Burt Rutan is twenty-eight years older than Elon Musk—they share remarkably similar stories of being inspired by Space exploration. Nearly all grew up watching *Star Trek*; all of them talk about watching the Apollo missions as a life-changing experience; all of them are STEM geeks; and all of them wish to inspire a younger generation to go into Space.

# A REMARKABLE RESEMBLANCE:
# OUTER SPACE AND VIRTUAL SPACE

In fact, the Space industry bears a remarkable resemblance to an industry that enriched most Space entrepreneurs: the Internet, another space that's virtually out of this world. A generation ago, few people imagined that the "brick and mortar" world of retail would be rocked by an online bookstore named after a river, or that people would trust their money to flow through a place called PayPal, or that computer geeks would become billionaire celebrities while still in their twenties.

Those web and software entrepreneurs defied the establishment in every way possible; Steve Jobs, Bill Gates, and Mark Zuckerberg were proud college dropouts who spent their careers defying expectations and achieving the impossible. Although Elon Musk differed in that he earned two bachelor's degrees, the sheer age in which he made a name for himself defied conventional norms. He didn't just become rich in his twenties, he founded and sold two successful companies while in his twenties, and went on to create three companies in three years, all in different industries: Space, automotive, and solar energy.

Just as Apollo inspired a generation of technically minded people, the Internet generation attracted the best and the brightest to explore their own virtual worlds. But these web pioneers were also inspired by the Space pioneers who went to the moon. When the time came to put their vast new wealth to the highest purpose possible, entrepreneurs like Bezos, Musk, and Ansari understandably chose Space. "Astronauts were like heroes to them," said John Spencer, president of the Space Tourism Society, in an interview with *Entrepreneur* magazine. "Once they grew up and became wealthy enough, they migrated essentially to the Space world because that's the ultimate challenge."

Space is the coolest, noblest, next-level thing there is: a cornucopia of impossibilities to overcome, just like the early Internet.

There's another tie to the analogy between the Internet and Space: their initial dependence on government. The Internet began as ARPANET, a computer network among research universities set up by the Defense Department. The original satellites, which vastly increased the speed of communications between those computers, were sent up by NASA. It's no exaggeration to say that, without the government's original efforts in networking, microelectronics, and satellites, Bezos, Musk, Ansari, and Jobs would have had to make their money elsewhere. There would be no Internet as we know it.

Similarly, Space entrepreneurs depended on the government's pioneering efforts in research, risk-taking, and contracts. But the point here is not to disparage private Space ventures. On the contrary, their initial dependence on NASA and the Defense Department shows how government can stimulate the next generation's economic and technological innovations. The American economy, a phenomenon unprecedented in history, was built by both public and private efforts. Private Space ventures are carving out niches in Space, only one or two of which overlap with NASA's continuing efforts. While Elon Musk continues to set the lofty goal of a private Mars colony, most of the entrepreneurial ventures in Space are limited to the area between Earth and lower orbital paths around it. Private ventures focus on five basic areas: tourism, satellites, research, and—speculatively—Space mining and suborbital travel. Currently, the Space industry alone constitutes a $300 billion-plus sector that has been growing at a healthy annual pace of 4.9 percent.

# LAUNCHPAD

1. What and/or who inspires you?

2. What other organizations or new industries are a result of the Space program?

3. Like the Internet and Space, education depends on the government. What are the advantages of these ties? How does this relationship impede the progress of education as a system?

4. How might the knowledge and technology that is developed through Space programs impact career opportunities of the future, specifically in the private venture areas of tourism, satellites, research, mining, and suborbital travel?

5. Visit spacetourismsociety.org and consider how Space exploration will continue to impact the tourism industry. How does this impact how we prepare students for their future?

Elon Musk built an industrial empire from the stuff of little boy dreams: fast cars and rocket ships. Musk is an idealist who told us he had to start his company so that man could colonize Mars and save the Earth. His sister says it's like her brother traveled into the future and came back to tell us all about it.

**SCOTT PELLEY**
*CBS News report*

# CHAPTER SIXTEEN

# Space Entrepreneurship

**T**HE BIGGEST REGRETS IN life are usually not about what we did, but what we didn't do. This is not the case for Elon Musk. He didn't expect Tesla to succeed. In fact, he was confident that the first of the SpaceX rockets wouldn't make it back from orbit, or even launch in the first place. Many people have an important idea but do not bother to try it, because of a lack of belief in self, the fear of failing, or the inability to articulate that idea in a way that garners support.

Elon Musk, the man behind the successful launch of PayPal, and the inspiration for Robert Downey Jr.'s portrayal of Iron Man, learned that Space exploration is even more challenging than cyberspace. An achiever accustomed to impossible goals, Musk was all of twenty-eight years old when he sold his first software company for $309 million. He was thirty-one when he sold PayPal to eBay for $1.5 billion. Several months before that sale, in June 2002, he founded SpaceX. In just seven years, the company rapidly built the Falcon 1, named after the *Millennium Falcon* from *Star Wars*, along with the Dragon spacecraft, designed to carry both cargo and humans. The progress was impressive, though slower than Musk had hoped as he had planned to put a vehicle on Mars by 2010.

In 2006, after Musk sank a total of $100 million of his own money into the business, NASA awarded it a $278 million contract to develop technology for servicing the International Space Station; and an additional agreement raised the total to $396 million. The deal stipulated that the rockets and spacecraft actually had to work, but the Falcon's first three launches failed. Meanwhile, SpaceX was spending $4 million a month on unproven technology. By 2008, the company was not only in trouble, it was threatening to bring down Musk's other ventures: the Tesla electric car and SolarCity, a company that makes solar power systems and charging stations for electric vehicles.

In 2008, Elon Musk was on a fourth attempt and running on financial fumes when he received a call from NASA, during the week of Christmas, informing him that his company had a $1.6 billion contract to ferry supplies to the International Space Station. NASA orders to date have totaled $3 billion—thirty times Musk's personal investment in SpaceX.

The week of Christmas seems to play a theme in his success. On December 22, 2015, the first stage of a rocket called Falcon 9 helped drive a payload of eleven satellites into low Earth orbit, then, thirty-five seconds later, executed a ballet of engine burns and stuck its landing just five miles from the launch pad on Cape Canaveral. The first rocket with an orbital payload that managed to return for a successful upright landing, Falcon 9 was a triumph for SpaceX—for its brilliant founder Elon Musk, for the teams of scientists and engineers, and for the cause of commercial Space.

The moment was significant for more than the technology. SpaceX had succeeded in proving the practicability of relatively low-cost Space flight. If it hadn't been for direct government support, and the knowledge gained from NASA's previous missions, the SpaceX, Blue Origin, and Virgin Galactic rockets would never have left the ground.

Just a few days before Christmas of 2017, SpaceX marveled the world with the launch of Falcon 9, dropping ten satellites into their intended orbits. Watch the awe-inspiring footage here: space.com/39197-spacex-spectacular-rocket-launch-views.html.

"SpaceX has had a phenomenal year, and they've motivated and inspired a lot of people as to what is possible," said Eric Stallmer, president of the Commercial Spaceflight Federation, an industry group for the private Space sector. Want to inspire students to go into STEM? Get their heads in the clouds. The sky is no longer the limit!

# LAUNCHPAD

1. Think of success stories in which the individual had to overcome enormous odds or defeats in order to achieve great things. How can you apply these lessons in your own life?

2. Elon Musk launched two impossible companies, Tesla and SpaceX. What impossible ideas have you thought of pursuing? Are you pursuing them? If not, what has held you back?

3. Learning by doing is invaluable in the Martian Classroom, as is learning by failure. What are the biggest lessons you've learned as a result of failing? What adjustments need to be made in the education system to allow for more learning by failing?

We create the future by
educating those who want to
build it.

**STEPHEN SANDFORD**

# CHAPTER SEVENTEEN

# Red Alert!
# The Race to Space
# in Education

**S**PUTNIK WAS MORE THAN a simple satellite beeping into Space; it was a wake up call. It was a warning signal that the technology possessed by Russia was strong enough to launch bombs onto United States soil. Fingers immediately pointed at schools and educators, leading to an overhaul in not only science and engineering, but education as a whole.

When the Space Race began in 1957 with the launch of Sputnik 1, the American public had already entered a new era of technological marvels: affordable automobiles, color televisions becoming the norm, the interstate highway system, more than 1,000 computers built and sold, the development of a polio vaccine. We were on top of the world, technologically.

When the Soviets leapfrogged us into Space, with advances that could someday be used to destroy us, America had no choice but to begin the hard work of proving its technological resilience. The response went beyond increased defense spending on technology. For the first time, the nation saw education as a form of national security. The National Defense Education Act, or NDEA, increased funding for education at all levels by more than $1 billion, introduced low-interest student loans for higher education, and added a bevy of scholarship opportunities. Curricula in public schools became more challenging, with a new emphasis on math and science. Educators introduced many teaching tools that have influenced today's practices, including hands-on laboratory classes, overhead projectors (which have now been replaced by interactive whiteboards), and educational films (that have advanced into many forms of multimedia to bring multiple experts into any classroom).

The Space program did more than prove our technological leadership. It spawned an interest in STEM subject areas. Franklin Chang-Díaz remembers looking for Sputnik in Costa Rica when he was seven years old and being inspired to devote his life to Space. After being told in a letter from Wernher von Braun, then-director of the Marshall Space Flight Center, that he needed to study engineering and learn to fly if he wanted to be an astronaut, Chang-Díaz emigrated to the United States at eighteen, received a BS in mechanical engineering and a doctorate in physics, became an American citizen, and now holds the record (along with Jerry L. Ross) for most spaceflights—seven shuttle missions.

The lure was more than just Space; it was about the future. A revived public Space program is the change we need today to inspire the next generation of STEM students, teachers, and professionals. The future has always been linked to our identity as a nation. We could always make things better, and whatever it took, we were going to do that work. Now that we have achieved beyond the wildest dreams of our ancestors, the rate of acceleration seems to be slowing. Will it take another Sputnik to jar us to action?

Just as Sputnik led to Apollo and a burst of growth in STEM areas, a robust Space mission to put people on Mars in twenty years is the inspiration needed to revive STEM. This effort will ensure that we will have all the scientists and technologists needed. Why would this succeed? Kids are natural explorers and are inspired by Space to study science, technology, engineering, and math, and the advances through new discoveries which continue to be developed through Space exploration, along with the opportunity to solve big problems impacting our world. Strangely enough, the seemingly impossible task of going to Mars happens to be the most accessible, most achievable path to a future we can look forward to. That future is up to us.

More importantly, our best future doesn't happen without STEM. We create the future by educating those who want to build it. Space, and the lure of exploring new frontiers, is the *wow factor* that makes STEM cool and appealing.

# LAUNCHPAD

1. What technology do you use in your learning space that is different than what would be found in a pre-Sputnik classroom?

2. How have teaching methods changed over this time period?

3. Most feel that education is overdue for another overhaul, yet many conflicting ideas exist on what this should look like. Should an overhaul take place at a national level, in districts, schools, or in independent classrooms?

There can be no life without change, and to be afraid of what is different or unfamiliar is to be afraid of life.

**PRESIDENT THEODORE ROOSEVELT**

# WHAT'S NEXT?

**H**OW MIGHT WE SET our nation's Space program on a trajectory that would inspire not just the international community, but our youth in America? Using the Martian Classroom as a launchpad, we can begin to address this question.

Today we are well on the way toward a developed economy in low Earth orbit. Farther out, NASA missions can deliver outposts at the Lagrangian points, the moon, Mars, and asteroids, all within the next generation of students, but only if we intentionally take on this great task. A full effort will guarantee a dramatic uptick in the number of students in math, engineering, science, and technology. And it will nurture highly paid workers who will drive our economy well into the future. In short, the drawing power of Space must be utilized strategically.

We have come a long way in technological advances and Space travel, but in order to ensure that our great nation leads the way in future missions, we have to think bigger. The types of jobs we are preparing kids for, both on or off world, will still include many of the same needs that we have today, but will look drastically different. Doctors will not become obsolete, but technology will drastically change and improve healthcare and how it is done. We will still need transportation; however, it will look drastically different. Many industries will become digitized and jobs will become automated, but many more jobs will be created that do not exist today.

Education has always been about the future. Just as we have made great strides in industry and technology, we have made great strides in our advances in education. But as the very nature of work continues to morph, education has to morph as well. In this age of disruption and iteration, education leaders cannot rely on the way things have always been done. Technology has had a huge impact on every industry, yet many schools still do not have computer science or coding classes. This is a huge problem, as every field has been impacted by computers and will continue to become more reliant on technology.

> *"When we started the Space Task Group in 1958 I don't think any of us appreciated what we were up to, where we were going, what it was going to result in, the impact on the country, the impact on the world."*
>
> —Christopher C. Kraft,
> first flight director and retired NASA engineer

Mission Control Center is now named after Christopher Kraft, who played a pivotal role in developing the concept of a flight control center. I (Rachael) was struck by this quote as it's fascinating to think that at the time, the very people who put man on the moon, and developed technology that changed the very fabric of our society, didn't fully realize the impact that they would have on the world. When I think about the leadership that it takes to move the needle forward in education, to draw more students into CTE and STEM, we too do not fully appreciate the task before us and the impact we will have on the world.

## NEXT STEPS FOR SHAPING THE FUTURE

- Read *The Gravity Well: America's Next, Greatest Mission.*

- Become a thought leader on education progress and issues.

- Invite Rachael or Stephen to present a talk or keynote at your next education event.

- Take advantage of the significant educational material provided by NASA.

- Visit MartianClassroom.org and subscribe to the site's blog updates for the latest ideas for The Martian Classroom.

- Be an advocate for education and communicate with your representatives in congress. On Congress.gov, you can find the contact information and voting records of your representatives and senators.

- Contact a NASA Center. Each center has resources specifically designed for educators. Here are a few of the most notable programs:

  » Human Exploration Rover Challenge: High-school and college teams of six must design, build, and race a human-powered rover through an obstacle course designed to simulate the terrain of rocky planets like Mars.

  » NASA Student Launch: Teams design and launch high-powered rockets to study propulsion systems. Varying challenges are offered to students from middle school through graduate school, as well as nonacademic teams

  » The FIRST Robotics Competition: High-school teams of twenty-five or more students have six weeks to build and program a robot to complete challenging tasks against competitors. NASA funds this.

» Sally Ride Center EarthKAM: In this NASA educational outreach program, middle-school students can request images of specific locations on Earth taken from Space. Sally Ride, the first woman in Space, founded this project in 1995.

- Visit acteonline.org for advocacy and educational resources for CTE and for resources on "STEM is CTE" symposiums.

- Visit 100kin10.org to provide input and support in addressing the nation's shortage of STEM teachers and to help solve the challenges that inhibit STEM learning.

Expand your out-of-this world
vocabulary with these terms
and suggest ones to add
using #MartianClassroom on
social media!

# APPENDIX

# Terminology for the Martian Classroom

**HERE'S AN ALPHABETICAL LISTING OF** a handful of terms, followed by some questions for your Martian classroom discussion.

## Aeronautics

Takeoff and landing are the most thrilling part of a trip on an airplane (next to the "free" snacks, of course). The word "aeronautics" means the science of flight, including the operation of flying machines. In your Martian classroom, you can start exploring more than just planes, but spaceships and much more.

## Algae

Yes, it's the green slimy stuff we find in wet areas. It's the goop that causes us to slip and slide on the rocks in the river or the ocean. So why is algae included in the list of vocabulary for the Martian Classroom? Some of the varieties of photosynthetic organisms constituting algae could provide oxygen and food on long-traveling spaceships. Forget peanuts, did I just hear sushi and seaweed snacks? Bon appétit!

## Ames Research Center (ARC)

Conducts critical research and develops enabling technologies in astrobiology, information technology, fundamental Space biology, nanotechnology, air-traffic management, thermal protection systems, and human factors essential to virtually all NASA missions. Wait—what was that again? The research that happens in this Silicon Valley Research Center contributes to **virtually every NASA mission!** If you want to hear highlights from conversations with the scientists, researchers, engineers, and astronauts in 2017, tune into this podcast: nasa.gov/ames/nisv-podcast-2017-end-of-year.

## Arianespace

A French multinational corporation and commercial Space service provider. Visit arianespace.com for completed missions and stunning images. While on the site, be sure to watch their latest success, the launch of Ariane Flight VA240 with four Galileo satellites. From the coverage of the 2017 solar eclipse to the center's supersonic research, explore the latest milestones on the Arianespace website.

## Asteroid Belt

An asteroid is a relatively small, inactive, rocky body that orbits the sun. Lying between Mars and Jupiter, the asteroid belt space contains a large percentage of the asteroids in our Solar System. According to NASA (jpl.nasa.gov/asteroidwatch/fastfacts.php), an asteroid the size of an automobile enters the Earth's atmosphere and burns up before reaching the surface, creating a fireball. A meteoroid the size of a football field hits Earth every 2,000 years or so, causing significant damage to the area. Talk about a touchdown! In February of 2013, a sixty-six-foot-wide asteroid broke up over Chelyabinsk, Russia, shattering glass and injuring more than 1,200 people. This incident resulted in the creation of the European Space Agency, with an asteroid warning center among other initiatives.

## Astronomical Unit (AU)

A standard Space measurement based on the distance between Earth and the Sun—some 93 million miles, or one AU. This makes the numbers smaller and easier to work with.

## Christopher C. Kraft Mission Control Center

Named after the first flight director and retired NASA engineer, this facility is located at the Lyndon B. Johnson Space Center in Houston, Texas, and controlled most of the Apollo and Gemini missions, and Space Shuttle missions through STS-53.

## Cosmology

Not to be confused with cosmetology, cosmology is the study of the universe, including its origins. According to NASA, it is "the scientific study of the large scale properties of the universe as a whole" and includes puzzling concepts such as string theory, dark matter, and even the fate of the universe. The average base salary for a cosmologist in the United States is $83,000 (salaryexpert.com/salary/job/cosmologist/united-states) and the rewards are endless!

## Deep Space Network (DSN)

A global communications network, including large antennas, to support missions beyond the moon.

## Department of Defense (DOD)

The largest employer in the world, this executive branch department of the United States federal government is charged with overseeing national security and the United States Armed Forces.

## Energetic Particle

Radiation capable of penetrating the walls of spacecraft, including gamma rays and X-rays.

## Escape Velocity

In society, we have maximum speeds. In physics, we have minimum speeds. The minimum velocity allows an object or vehicle to escape gravity. The escape velocity for Earth's Gravity Well is 25,000 miles per hour.

## European Space Agency (ESA)

A consortium consisting of Austria, Belgium, Denmark, Finland, France, Germany, Ireland, Italy, the Netherlands, Norway, Portugal, Spain, Sweden, Switzerland, and the United Kingdom. Canada is an affiliate.

## Extravehicular Mobility Unit (EMU)

A two-piece spacesuit that allows an astronaut to live and communicate outside a spacecraft. Although the suit is a spacecraft in and of itself, it allows astronauts to work outside of a spacecraft, also known as a spacewalk. Visit the Interactive Spacesuit Experience at NASA.gov to get a better understanding of what it's like to be in an EMU.

## Exoplanets

Planets that are located outside of our Solar System. Explore an interactive gallery of the intriguing and exotic planets discovered so far: Exoplanet Exploration Program (exoplanets.nasa.gov).

## Gamma-Ray burst (GRB)

A shower of high-energy radiation that generally lasts just a few seconds, but could damage the DNA of astronauts outside Earth's magnetic field.

## GEO

Geosynchronous or geostationary orbit, in which a satellite, vehicle, or other object moves at the same speed as Earth's rotation. This "holds" the satellite in the same relative point above a spot on Earth. Weather satellites in GEO above Earth's equator "hover" at a distance of 22,300 miles above the surface.

## Glenn Research Center (GRC)

An Ohio-based NASA center that transfers critical technologies that address national priorities through research, technology development, and systems development for safe and reliable aeronautics, aerospace, and Space applications.

## Goddard Space Flight Center (GSFC)

One of the chief NASA laboratories, as well as the control center for the Hubble Space Telescope and other systems. Goddard is located in Maryland outside of Washington, DC.

## The Gravity Well

A deep hole in Space, a force that presses us to Earth, an obstacle stretching a million miles up and out, with us at the bottom. The Gravity Well also poses our generation's biggest obstacle and most promising challenge, a new frontier to explore, tame, and domesticate.

## Habitable Zone

A region in Space where planets contain liquid water, between the boiling and freezing points. Seven Earth-sized planets have recently been discovered, three of which are in the habitable zone. This planetary system is called TRAPPIST-1.

## Hubble Space Telescope (HST)

A powerful telescope in low Earth orbit since 1990. Hubble boasts an eight-foot mirror as well as four instruments that measure light from celestial objects in visible, near-ultraviolet, and near-infrared wavelengths. Take a peek at the mesmerizing collection of images taken from the HST: Hubble Space Telescope Images on NASA.gov.

## Intelsat

Originally an international organization of eleven nations, now a private company providing satellite service to more than 149 countries. Intelsat operates more than fifty communications satellites.

## Inverse Square Law

Any relation where the force between objects (like gravity) decreases with the square of the distance between them. A spacecraft 6,000 miles from Earth experiences one-quarter of the gravitational pull that it would 3,000 miles from the planet.

## Jet Propulsion Laboratory (JPL)

One of NASA's chief centers, based in Pasadena, California, and operated by the California Institute of Technology (Caltech). JPL develops and operates robotic spacecraft, including the Mars rovers, among other projects.

## Johnson Space Center (JSC)

The headquarters for human Space flight, in Houston, Texas.

## Kennedy Space Center (KSC)

Named after President John F. Kennedy and located on the east coast of Florida, Kennedy is NASA's main launch center for human Space flight. It also conducts launches for a variety of NASA missions.

## Lagrangian Point

A "flat" part of Space terrain, where a satellite or station can remain in place relative to two bodies, without expending energy. Five such points exist between the Sun and Earth. L1 and L2, the most potentially useful points for Space exploration, each lie a distance from Earth equal to four times the distance of the moon. Space.com (space.com/30302-lagrange-points.html) refers to these points as "Parking Places in Space."

## Langley Research Center (LaRC)

Based in coastal Virginia, Langley served as the original laboratory for NACA, NASA's predecessor. Langley conducts aeronautics and Space research for aerospace, atmospheric sciences, and technology commercialization.

## Low Earth Orbit (LEO)

A region in Space eighty-nine to 1,200 miles above Earth. What's so special about low Earth orbit? For one, it's the first step into Space.

## Magnetosphere

A region around a planet where the magnetic field controls the motions of charged particles. Earth's magnetosphere deflects or traps radiation that would otherwise prove deadly to most species, including humans. Leaving the magnetosphere presents one of the great challenges to human Space flight beyond the Gravity Well.

## Marshall Space Flight Center (MSFC)

A NASA center in Huntsville, Alabama, that conducts research, designs and builds rockets, and manages Space labs.

## Medium Earth Orbit (MEO)

The region between low Earth orbit and geosynchronous orbit, 1,200 to 22,000 miles from Earth.

## Microgravity
The condition of free fall, when an object appears to be weightless. Microgravity in Space allows the formation of precise crystals, along with other forms of manufacture and experimentation that would be near impossible on Earth.

## NACA
The National Advisory Committee for Aeronautics, NASA's predecessor.

## NASA
NASA stands for National Aeronautics and Space Administration. NASA was started in 1958 as a part of the United States government and is charged with overseeing science and technology in relation to airplanes or Space (nasa.gov/audience/forstudents/k-4/stories/nasa-knows/what-is-nasa-k4.html).

## Optics
The branch of physics that studies the properties of light.

## Speed of Light
The speed at which photons move through empty Space, about 186,000 miles per second.

## Sputnik
The first artificial satellite to successfully enter Earth's orbit. Sputnik (history.nasa.gov/sputnik/sputorig.html) marked the dawn of the Space Age and the Space Race as the United States scrambled to regain its status as the leading nation. Termed the "Sputnik Effect," (edweek.org/ew/articles/2007/10/02/06bracey_web.h27.html) fingers quickly pointed toward education as the culprit for the Soviet Union's lead, thus leading to endless education reforms in an effort to regain technological ground.

## Stennis Space Center

Stennis is responsible for NASA's rocket-propulsion testing and for partnering with industry to develop and implement remote-sensing technology.

## Van Allen Belts

A pair of high-radiation bands trapped by Earth's magnetic field, as close as 500 miles and as far as 40,000 miles from Earth.

# LAUNCHPAD

1. What food products contain algae? Explore algae recipes and find ones that you would enjoy dining on for a long voyage through Space.

2. In 2015, Arianespace assured the French parliament that it could outcompete SpaceX and proved that it could surpass SpaceX in commercial launch orders. Who do you think is currently leading the competition?

3. In 2012, the Astronomical Unit was redefined, simplifying a confusing calculation into a single number. What other systems or even social constructs could use an overhaul?

4. If a physical location were to be named after you, what would it be, where, and why?

5. Visit the "Dress Me for Space" Play and Learn at NASA.gov for a fun and interactive way to teach grades kindergarten through four about Extravehicular Mobility Units.

6. Dig deeper: Beyond the definition provided in this section, what is the Gravity Well, and what promises are held within?

7. What is the significance of the treasure trove of planets found, three of which are in the habitable zone?

8. Visit NASA.gov for a free resource to use with grades five through twelve to help students understand how the brightness of light can be used to measure distances to stars and far away galaxies: the Inverse Square Law of Light.

9. What are the physical consequences of light-speed travel? nasa.gov/audience/foreducators/topnav/materials/listbytype/Inverse_Square.html.

10. Where did the Stennis Space Center get its name?

11. The discovery of the Van Allen belts is credited to James Van Allen. How did he come across this discovery, and why does it matter?

Around here, however, we don't look backwards very long. We keep moving forward, opening new doors and doing new things, because we're curious ... and curiosity keeps leading us down new paths.

**WALT DISNEY**

# MISSIONS FOR THE MARTIAN CLASSROOM

How do the Mission to Mars and other aspects of exploration connect to your content area?

Hint: The Space program can be linked to all subjects in ways that are both grounded to Earth and out of this world! Space isn't just for science class. It can and should be connected to every subject and grade level. Here are some ideas to get started:

- ❋ Instead of bellwork, have a launch assignment. A simple tweak to the structure of a lesson, such as the title of an activity, can transform the level of excitement about the learning that is about to take place.

- ௸ Are objectives written on the board when students arrive to class? Congratulations, the building administrator is undoubtedly applauding. The students, on the other hand, are bored to tears by the words "students will be able to." Why not turn the objectives into destinations? Students then determine when they have "arrived" by demonstrating learning for mastery.

⚙ Human nature longs for a challenge. This is why we are drawn to competitions; whether sports, video games, or NASA challenges. When introducing potential careers to students, start with the line, "Do you have what it takes to be a _____?" in place of the standard titles of "requirements" or "qualifications." The simple phrase, "Do you have what it takes?" gives students something to aspire to and gives motivation and inspiration to obtain the necessary skill sets.

♁ Along the same lines, get students involved in NASA challenges. Visit NASA's "Get Involved: NASA Solve" (nasa.gov/solve/opportunities) for opportunities to explore and solve challenges around topics such as information technology, citizen science, multimedia production, engineering and modeling, aeronautics, and more. Other challenges include art contests and even "Train Like an Astronaut: Walk to the Moon" to encourage healthy lifestyles. The NASA HUNCH, or High School Students United with NASA to Create Hardware, is a favorite with its Culinary Challenge component.

✳ Teach language arts and history through a biography of Neil Armstrong (biography.com/people/neil-armstrong-9188943). Take this a step further and create a drama assignment where students act out scenes from the biography. As a bonus, give them the option of writing the biography of the first person to step foot on Mars.

⊚ The NASA Art Program (nasa.gov/feature/nasa-and-art-a-collaboration-colored-with-history) blurs the lines between science, history, the future, and art as it commemorates both past events and interpretations of future events and discoveries. Explore the NASA History Flickr page and ask students to write a story about one of the images. Have students research a Space mission and create their own visual representation of their learning.

⚙ Tourism will morph into a whole new map as we continue to explore new frontiers. Visit alien worlds on the NASA

Exoplanet Exploration website (exoplanets.nasa.gov) for downloadable posters for the classroom. While there, check out the "Universe of Monsters" and "Galaxy of Horrors" with your students to get creative juices flowing.

⚖ Get students writing about Space. Science on the Space Station is coordinated by CASIS, the Center for the Advancement of Science in Space (iss-casis.org/about/about-the-iss-national-lab). The entity has funded and facilitated experiments ranging from vascular tissue research to cell growth on scaffolds (known fondly as "organs on chips"), to fluid dynamics and remote sensing. CASIS also lets private businesses conduct experiments, and it forms partnerships with nonprofit organizations to spark interest in STEM.

» For example, Boy Scouts in the Chicago area (chicagotribune.com/suburbs/ct-boy-scout-experiment-for-space-station-met-20170811-story.html) sent microgravity experiments to the Space Station on August 8, 2017, to measure genetic mutations of bacteria in low gravity compared with the changes that occur on Earth in an attempt to find better ways to fight cancer. Have students read about this fascinating project and others like these and write a prediction on what they believe the outcomes will be, or about an experiment they would like to propose.

❈ Get students creating art about Space through monthly Space gallery art competitions with ESA Kids (esa.int/esaKIDSen/index.html). Explore this site for fun facts, activities, videos, and other contests about our universe.

◍ Teaching a class or unit on entrepreneurship? Have students develop and pitch a concept for a product or business that would be connected to low orbit, a mission to Mars, or beyond. Use Flipgrid (info.flipgrid.com) for students to pitch their idea in three minutes or less and send a link to the grid to business and industry partners to provide feedback to students.

⚙ Visit nasa.gov/realmartians for education resources to use in your classroom, such as "Nine Real NASA Technologies in *The Martian*."

⚗ Ask students to read the blog post, "Out-Of-This-World Careers That Do Not Require Take-Off" (martianclassroom.org/blog/earthboundspacejobs) and determine which of these would be the best fit for them and why.

❋ Creativity and play are common themes in innovation and can help solve big problems. Give students agency in demonstrating mastery of content in fun and creative ways, using a menu of options such as this:

## SHOW WHAT YOU KNOW LEARNING MENU

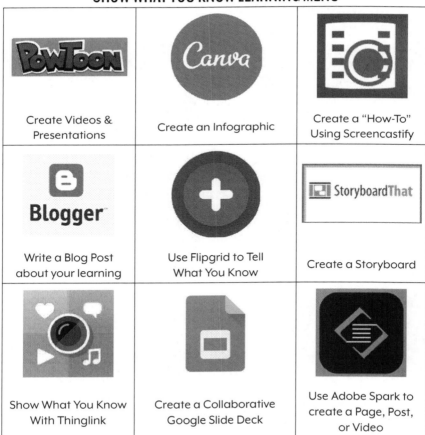

| | | |
|---|---|---|
| Create Videos & Presentations | Create an Infographic | Create a "How-To" Using Screencastify |
| Write a Blog Post about your learning | Use Flipgrid to Tell What You Know | Create a Storyboard |
| Show What You Know With Thinglink | Create a Collaborative Google Slide Deck | Use Adobe Spark to create a Page, Post, or Video |

# THE BOOKSHELVES OF THE MARTIAN CLASSROOM

Yes, there is such a thing as bookshelves in the Martian Classroom! Although filled with technology, online references, and cutting-edge resources, the Martian Classroom still has room for a shelf or two, and turning the pages of these must-have books. Or, if you prefer, most are available on Kindle or Audible. As you read through the list and think of ones to add, share your ideas with the community using the hashtag #MartianClassroom. Visit MartianClassroom.org for updates to this list of the best resources and links.

- *Beyond: Our Future in Space,* Chris Impey
- *Brain Rules: 12 Principles for Surviving and Thriving at Work, Home, and School,* John Medina
- *Business Dynamics: Systems Thinking and Modeling for a Complex World,* John D. Sterman
- *Creating Innovators: The Making of Young People Who Will Change the World,* Tony Wagner
- *Ditch That Textbook: Free Your Teaching and Revolutionize Your Classroom,* Matt Miller
- *Engineer in Charge: A History of the Langley Aeronautical Laboratory, 1917-1958,* James Hansen
- *Hidden Figures: The American Dream and the Untold Story of the Black Women Who Helped Win the Space Race,* Margot Lee Shetterly
- *Hidden Figures: The True Story of Four Black Women and the Space Race,* Margot Lee Shetterly
- *Originals: How Non-Conformists Move the World,* Adam Grant
- *Project Apollo: The Tough Decisions,* Robert Seamans, Jr.
- *Science, Truth and Democracy,* Philip Kitchner
- *Smarter: The New Science of Building Brain Power,* Dan Hurley
- *Space Chronicles: Facing the Ultimate Frontier,* Neil DeGrasse Tyson
- *The Ancient Economy,* M.I. Finley

- ÷ *The Darkest Dark*, Chris Hadfield and Kate Fillion
- ❋ *The Economics of Good and Evil: The Quest for Economic Meaning from Gilgamesh to Wall Street*, Tomas Sedlacek
- ⓖ *The Entrepreneurial State: Debunking Public vs. Private Sector Myths*, Mariana Mazzucato
- ⚙ *The Gravity Well: America's Next, Greatest Mission*, Stephen Sandford and Jay Heinrichs
- ÷ *The New Ocean: The Story of the First Space Age*, William E. Burrows
- ❋ *The One World Schoolhouse: Education Reimagined*, Salmon Khan
- ⓖ *The Privatization of Space Exploration: Business, Technology, Law, and Policy*, Lewis D. Solomon
- ⚙ *The Secret of Apollo: Systems Management in American and European Space Programs*, Stephen P. Johnson
- ÷ *The Talent Code*, Daniel Coyle
- ❋ *The Wealth and Poverty of Nations: Why Some Are So Rich and Some Are So Poor*, David S. Landes
- ⓖ *Thinking in Systems: A Primer*, Donella H. Meadows
- ⚙ *Von Braun: Dreamer of Space, Engineer of War*, Michael J. Neufeld
- ÷ *Why Nations Fail: The Origins of Power, Prosperity, and Poverty*, Daron Acemoglu and James Robinson

## APPS AND SITES FOR THE MARTIANS IN YOUR CLASSROOM

The Martian Classroom extends beyond the walls of a school building or the time constructs of a calendar year. Not even Mars itself poses a limit! Check out these resources to explore with kids of all ages. Fun is often authentic learning in disguise.

Here's our list of apps and websites to explore. Yes, they are free—except the ones that are not. The "$" symbol denotes a cost at the time that this book was written. Visit MartiansClassroom.org for updates to this list of the best resources and links.

# APPS

## NASA Be a Martian

This app lets you participate in the current (and future) missions on Mars, with the latest images and news.

> ❋ itunes.apple.com/us/app/nasa-be-a-martian/
> id543704769?mt=8

## Earth Now

Another app from the Jet Propulsion Laboratory. This one uses maps to visualize recent data from Earth science satellites, including surface-air temperature, carbon dioxide, carbon monoxide, ozone, and water vapor as well as gravity and sea level variations.

> ⓐ play.google.com/store/apps/details?id=gov.nasa.jpl.
> earthnow.activity

## Hour of Code Space Quest

Build a *Star Wars* galaxy with code.

> ⚙ hourofcode.com/star-wars

## Images of Change

This NASA app lets you see just how Earth is changing, including then-and-now comparisons of glaciers, wildfire sites, and floods.

> ÷ climate.nasa.gov/images-of-change

## ISS Live App

This app makes you feel a part of the International Space Station, with virtual 3D tours and live stream of data.

> ❋ play.google.com/store/apps/details?id=isslive.nadion.com

## ISS Spotter

Find out when the International Space Station will be visible from your roof or backyard, then set an alarm to make sure you can see it. The built-in compass will help your spotting.

⊚ itunes.apple.com/us/app/iss-spotter/id523486350?mt=8

## Lucianna

American Girl partnered with NASA to introduce Luciana in 2018, an inspiring character who wants to be the first person to step foot on Mars. Visit the American Girl app for out-of-this world videos and Space activities, including augmented reality.

⚙ play.americangirl.com/play/girl-of-the-year/luciana

## NASA 365

NASA events and trivia for each day of the year. See what happened in Space on your birthday.

⊕ play.google.com/store/apps/details?id=gov.nasa.neacc.
   space365

## NASA App

Get the latest agency news, find the NASA facility nearest you, and watch a seemingly infinite number of videos and images.

✳ nasa.gov/nasaapp

## NASA Be a Martian

This app lets you participate in the current (and future) missions on Mars, with the latest images and news.

⊚ itunes.apple.com/us/app/nasa-be-a-martian/
   id543704769?mt=8

## NASA Spinoff

NASA Spinoff profiles the best examples of technology that have been transferred from NASA research and missions into commercial products.

From life-saving satellite systems to hospital robots that care for patients and more, NASA technologies benefit society. There's more Space in your life than you think!

⚙ itunes.apple.com/us/app/nasa-spinoff-2013/
   id904717045?mt=8

## New Horizons App

Explore Pluto and the outer Solar System through images from NASA's probe.

÷ pluto.jhuapl.edu/epoapps

## Rocket Science 101

This app, created by NASA's Launch Services Program, lets you build your own rocket for your favorite NASA mission.

❋ itunes.apple.com/us/app/rocket-science-101/
   id536290350?mt=8

## Sol 0: Mars Colonization

This is an online real-time strategy game for students to establish the first Martian colony using technology that may be available in the years to come.

◉ $ store.steampowered.com/app/387370/
   Sol_0_Mars_Colonization

## Space, Astronomy & NASA News

NASA's one-stop app for the latest Space news.

⚙ itunes.apple.com/us/app/space-nasa-astronomy-news/
   id938121601?mt=8

## Space Images App

This picture-packed app lets you share the most amazing images on social media.

÷ jpl.nasa.gov/apps

# WEBSITES

## The Alliance for Space Development

This organization advocates settlements in Space.

✳ allianceforspacedevelopment.org

## Amazing Space

The best astronomy site on the Web. If you're interested in the Hubble or James Webb Telescopes, here is where you'll find the latest data and images.

◉ amazingspace.org

## ESA

This site contains the latest news from across the "pond."

⚙ esa.int

## Google's $30 Million X Prize

This program spurs innovation in low-cost robotic commercial Space exploration. As you might expect from Google, this site is very, very cool, including a documentary series produced by J.J. Abrams of *Star Wars* and *Star Trek* fame.

÷ lunar.xprize.org

## NASA

NASA.gov is one of the least stuffy government websites, packed with multimedia. This is the place to learn how to participate directly with Space, from getting your scout troop's experiment onto the International Space Station to visiting the Johnson Space Center.

✳ nasa.gov

## NASA Space Place

NASA Space Place is a fun site for kids, with everything Space and NASA.

◉ spaceplace.nasa.gov

## National Space Society
The site of the National Space Society, which advocates human colonization of Space.

⚙ nss.org

## Planetary Society
The site for the Planetary Society, Mars Society, SETI Institute, Commercial Spaceflight Federation, and the Coalition for Deep Space Exploration.

÷ planetary.org

## Space.com
Space.com is a great source of information, gathered by a commercial online publisher, and has news of the latest commercial and government launches, astronomy facts, and even an area where you can shop for a telescope.

✳ space.com

## Space Daily
Space Daily is the go-to site for Space news. While geared toward the true Space fan, Space Daily works on the brain the way baseball does. Follow the players and the games (or, in this case, missions), and you might find yourself becoming a true fanatic.

◉ spacedaily.com

## The Space Foundation
The Space Foundation leads educational programs and holds an annual symposium of Space stakeholders.

⚙ spacefoundation.org

## The Space Telescope Science Institute
The Space Telescope Science Institute is located within Johns Hopkins University. Get a close look at missions run by this inside player.

÷ stsci.edu

## Space Weather

Space weather affects telecommunications on Earth, and it can affect the timing of launches. It's a cool way to see how the Sun impacts Earth with its cosmic rays.

　❋　spaceweather.com

## SpaceX

Visit SpaceX to keep up with Elon Musk's ventures in space.

　◉　spacex.com

# SPACE FACTS AND STATS

## Space Terrain

- If you look at some maps of Space between the Sun and Mars, with Earth in between, the blackness of Space is intersected with curved lines that look a lot like a topographic map of a wilderness on Earth. (The website ScienceArt.com contains some of the most beautiful images.)

- Lagrangian points are the "flat" places in Space where the pulling and pushing forces are in balance. The orbiting object constantly pushes away from one body, held back by gravity, while the pulling of a second body keeps the object in the same place relative to the two large bodies. (Paul A. Tipler, *Elementary Modern Physics,* Chapter 9: Astrophysics and Cosmology)

- Each pair of bodies in the Solar System has five Lagrangian points between them. (Space.com has a good review of our Solar System's Lagrangian points. Search the site for "Lagrange Points." Also see NASA Earth Observatory, EarthObservatory. nasa.gov.)

- Venus used to be a pleasant, watery, habitable planet much like ours. The Martian atmosphere, it turns out, also used to be much more like Earth's. Both planets built up carbon dioxide, trapping the Sun's rays and causing the planets to warm dramatically.

(Fredric W. Taylor, *The Scientific Exploration of Venus;* Giles Sparrow, *Mars*)

## Looking Back

- The first commercial flight took place on New Year's Day, 1914, with a ticket price of $400. That's over $10,000 in today's money. It carried a single passenger from St. Petersburg to Tampa, Florida. (Tim Sharp, "World's First Commercial Airline," in space.com)

- In April 2001, Space Adventures sent American businessman Dennis Tito to the International Space Station for a reported $20 million payment, making him the first Space tourist.

- At the height of the attempt to send men to the moon—when NASA sent three humans 25,000 miles an hour into Space, circled the moon, and brought them back safely—most citizens opposed the program. (Herbert E. Krugman, "Public Attitudes Toward the Apollo Space Program, 1965– 1975," *Journal of Communication,* December 1977)

- On July 20, 1969, an estimated 600 million people around the globe watched Neil Armstrong take his first steps onto the lunar surface. This was about fifteen percent of everyone alive at that time. ("When the Eagle Landed," *Wall Street Journal,* July 16, 2009)

- Three years passed between the first transcontinental airmail service and the establishment of the first transcontinental airline. ("Airmail creates an industry." *National Postal Museum,* Smithsonian, 2004; "From mail-sack seats to sleeping berths and above-cloud routes," Boeing Frontiers.)

- Twelve years passed between the Soviets' first rocket and the Americans' moon landing. (The R-7 intercontinental missile launched in 1957. The moon landing took place in 1969.)

- Eugene Cernan, commander of Apollo 17, holds the distinction of being the last person to set foot on the moon, December 14, 1972. (See the Smithsonian Air and Space Museum website, AirandSpace.si.edu.)

- The five Space Shuttles completed 135 missions over twenty-two years, until the program ended in 2011. (Piers Bizony, *The Space Shuttle*)

- Sixteen nations, including the United States, participated in building the International Space Station. (Conclusion in W. Henry Lambright, ed., *Space Policy in the 21st Century*.)

## NASA

- America's Space agency isn't just about Space. Its major initiatives comprise astrophysics (the purest science of the cosmos), study of our Solar System, aeronautics (focusing on improvements to aviation technology), Earth science, examination of the Sun, Space technology (which finds new ways to conduct robotic and human missions), and finally, the human exploration program. (nasa.gov)

- To bring humans and their equipment into Space, NASA is building its biggest rocket ever, the Space launch system. The first version will push seventy-seven tons into orbit. Eventually, the plan is to build a rocket that can carry 143 tons into Space—ten percent more thrust than the Saturn V. (AerospaceGuide.net)

- When Eisenhower created NASA, the highest earners in America were paying a top marginal tax rate of more than ninety percent; it is now just over thirty-nine percent. (TaxFoundation.org)

- Over the previous three decades, our nation's leaders have reduced NASA's buying power by twenty-five percent. (TheGuardian.com, Data Blog, "NASA Budgets: U. S. spending on Space travel since 1958 updated"; contains a chart showing budgets as well as NASA's portion of the federal budget.)

- The 2015 Space movie, *The Martian*, in which Matt Damon plays an astronaut-botanist, took in more box office receipts on its opening weekend than NASA's daily budget. (BoxOfficeMojo.com. The movie took in $54.3 million on its first weekend. NASA's daily budget is $52.8 million.)

- The amount NASA needs is comparable to someone with an income of $60,000 spending $10 annually on Space. (This rough estimate assumes a $30 billion NASA budget. Individual income taxes provide forty-seven percent of federal revenue, according to the Center on Budget and Policy Priorities. A person with a $60,000 income, no children, and no special circumstances pays $8,196.25, according to TaxFormCalculator.com.)

## Private Sector

- Elon Musk put up $100 million of his own money for SpaceX and received $1.25 billion in venture capital. NASA has awarded the company $3 billion in contracts. ("SpaceX overview on secondmarket," Secondmarket, a division of NASDAQ)

- It costs $50 million to $500 million to put a satellite into low Earth orbit. SpaceX promises a price per pound in low Earth orbit of $709—one-seventh the current price. (SpaceX.com. The company's stated cost of a Falcon Heavy rocket is $90 million; it carries a payload into low Earth orbit of almost 120,000 pounds. Motley Fool, fool.com, contains a list of commercial companies and the cost of launching satellites with each. Search for "How Much Does It Cost to Launch a Satellite?")

- Sixteen private companies compete in Space, along with three commercial wings of national Space agencies. (Wikipedia has an up-to-date list of companies. Search for "List of private Space companies.")

- The Apollo mission directed eighty-five percent of its budget—more than $100 million—to private companies. That percentage holds true to this day. (space.com)

- The private sector funds just eighteen percent of basic research in this country. The public sector funds fifty-seven percent, with universities and foundations covering the rest. (Mariana Mazzucato, *The Entrepreneurial State*. Also see the MIT report, "The Future Postponed: Why Declining Investment in Basic Research Threatens a U.S. Innovation Deficit," reported in BusinessInsider.com.)

- Federal employees constitute just twenty percent of the total NASA mission workforce. ("Employee Orientation," nasa.gov)

## The Gravity Well

- Most of today's Space economy occupies low Earth orbit, a 1,200-mile-wide band that's a slice of less than one one-thousandth of the Gravity Well. (Wikipedia has current information on satellites in LEO, MEO, and GEO. Search for "satellites.")

- To get into low Earth orbit—a path in which the forces of motion balance the pull of gravity—a rocket has to attain a speed of about 17,000 miles per hour. To escape the Gravity Well, a vehicle must go about 25,000 miles per hour—thirty-three times the speed of sound. (Daniel Fleisch and Julia Kregenow, *A Student's Guide to the Mathematics of Astronomy*)

- As a rule of thumb, ten pounds of rocket fuel are required to push one pound of equipment or human into low Earth orbit. (Howard E. McCurdy, *Faster, Better, Cheaper: Low-Cost Innovation in the U.S. Space Program*)

- At 240,000 miles on average, the moon lies only one-fifth of the way to the top of the Gravity Well. This is equal to about eighty Columbus voyages. But you need far more energy to get from Earth to the moon than from the moon to Mars. (Peter Cadogan, *The Moon—Our Sister Planet*)

- To travel to Mars, astronauts will have to complete about 8,750 Columbus voyages of distance, assuming that Mars and Earth are at their closest points in their respective orbits around the Sun, a position they take once every two years. While the distance is vast, the fuel cost is not as much as you'd expect; the terrain from the moon to Mars is milder than that from Earth to the moon. (Calculation based on Columbus's first voyage, from his journal, edited by Clements R. Markham.)

## Economy

- Aviation contributes $1.5 trillion—more than five percent—to the national economy. (Federal Aviation Administration, "The Economic Impact of Civil Aviation on the U.S. Economy," June 2014)

- The Apollo program led to the creation of the lightweight mini-computer, GPS, the kidney dialysis machine, the smoke detector, the rechargeable pacemaker, the CPAP breathing machine, advanced prosthetics, a lead paint detector, improved vehicle brakes, freeze-dried food, and camera-on-a-chip technology used in smartphones today. (Spinoff.nasa.gov)

- More than a thousand satellites occupy low Earth orbit, or LEO. (Programmer James Yoder has created a website that lets you see everything orbiting the Earth, including satellites and junk, in real time: StuffIn.space.)

- Several dozen satellites are in medium Earth orbit, or MEO, providing our GPS. (For a complete list of individual satellites, see gisgeography.com/free-satellite-imagery-data-list.)

- More than 250 satellites in geosynchronous orbit enable our Internet, television, and telephone communications. (Wikipedia has a current list of satellites in GEO. Search for "list of satellites in geosynchronous orbit.")

- The Space industry generates more than $300 billion in revenue, an amount that continues to grow five to fifteen percent a year. (Satellite Industry Association, sia.org)

- For every dollar spent on Space, the knowledge ore brings back as much as eight dollars. And that's not counting the 65,000 jobs created by the Space program—which uses private contractors to do most of the work. (The multiplier is an extrapolation from Jerome Schnee, "The Economic Impacts of the U.S. Space Program," available at er.jsc.nasa.gov.) The jobs figure is a conservative estimate, starting with the 18,000 NASA employees (nasa.gov) and tens of thousands of on-site contractors at NASA's Centers.

- Satellite-based weather tracking has an annual economic value of $11 billion. (Rodney F. Weiher, Chief Economist, NOAA)

- One asteroid can hold $20 trillion worth of minerals, more than the annual gross domestic product of the American economy. A small, one-hundred-foot asteroid can contain as much as $50 billion of platinum. (For a ranking of the value and mineral content of more than 600,000 asteroids, see asterank.com.)

# ACKNOWLEDGMENTS

**WE WOULD LIKE TO THANK** Jay Heinrichs, who helped crystallize the ideas for *The Gravity Well*. Thank you for sharing your expertise and for your desire to ensure a better future for the Martians in our classrooms. Jay Bennett, Lee Michaelides, and Miles Howard provided invaluable research on Space history, and fact-checked *The Gravity Well*, thus providing invaluable research for *The Martians in Your Classroom* as well. Kam Ghaffarian deserves special thanks for his vision and support for extending the original vision to the youngest generations.

To Holly Clark and Trevor MacKenzie, thank you for your insight and sharing tools to make this a reality. You have generously provided resources and feedback along with a healthy dose of inspiration.

Most importantly, we would like to acknowledge and thank the leaders that serve in the classrooms each day. Your role is truly the most important of all professions. You inspire the Martians in your learning spaces and fuel the desire to take on these great frontiers.

# ARE YOU READY TO LAUNCH?

## Get more fuel for your Martian classroom here.

**HERE ARE WAYS TO GET** more #MartianClassroom and #STEM ideas for your learning space:

- ❋ Visit martianclassroom.org for blog posts, resources, and to request Rachael Mann or Stephen Sandford to speak at your next event.
- ⓜ Follow us on Social Media!
  - » Twitter: @MartianEdu
  - » Instagram: @MartianClassroom
  - » #MartianClassroom

# POPULAR WORKSHOPS AND KEYNOTES INCLUDE:

## THE MARTIANS IN YOUR CLASSROOM

Sixty-six years separate the Wright Brothers from the Apollo 11 moon landing. The next great frontier is not too far away. The students in today's classrooms will not only witness colonies on the moon and Mars, they will also be the ones taking on these great frontiers and paving the way for humanity. How do we ensure that students are not only equipped for their future reality but that they are also the ones who create it? It comes down to CTE and STEM.

## TURNING IDEAS WORTH SPREADING INTO TALKS AND PRESENTATIONS

Memorable presentations do not happen by accident. Learn how the best presenters prepare for the stage and how to deliver your talk with confidence, whether speaking at a board meeting, parent-teacher conference, in an interview, or in the classroom. You will learn exercises to improve your performance and technology tools to help craft your next talk.

## EMPOWERING STUDENT VOICE

In this workshop, participants will learn the principles that all great communicators have in common, whether presenting on the stage or in 1-1 interactions. Participants will explore resources for teaching presentation literacy so that students know what to say, how to say it, and how to find the inner strength to use their voice with confidence. This session will provide you with free, online, easy-to-use resources to add to your presentation literacy toolkit. Learn how platforms like TED-Ed Clubs, Google Hangouts, Flipgrids, and more empower students to share their ideas and use their voice to make a positive impact on society at both the local and global levels.

## THE CULTURE IMPACT

What do Kool-Aid, yogurt, and Petri dishes have in common? They each hold clues for effective leadership in education. Discover how to create an environment that keeps your staff (and students) coming back for more.

## CREATING YOUR ONLINE, PROFESSIONAL BRAND

As our world becomes increasingly global, it is more important than ever to tap into virtual resources in a responsible manner to create your personal, professional brand, as well as to market your ideas and products. This session will equip you with the tools you need to establish a professional brand in order to stand apart from the masses and create a strong online presence in a connected world.

## EQUIPPING STUDENTS FOR RESPONSIBLE SOCIAL MEDIA USE

As our world becomes increasingly global, it is more important now than ever to train students to tap into virtual resources in a responsible manner to create their own personal, professional brand, as well as to market their ideas and products. This session will equip you with the tools you need to train students to establish a brand in order to stand apart from the masses and create a strong online presence.

## THERE'S A HAT FOR THAT

Educators wear many hats. Explore the many apps that will increase your effectiveness, for each hat that you wear, inside and outside of the classroom.

# FOR MORE INFORMATION OR TO REQUEST A WORKSHOP VISIT:

### Rachael Mann

- ⚙ RachaelMann.co
- ⚗ Twitter: @RachaelEdu
- ✳ Instagram: @RachaelEdu

### Stephen Sandford

- ⚲ thegravitywell.org
- ⚙ Twitter: @SPSandford
- ⚗ Instagram: @SPSandford

# BIBLIOGRAPHY

Beard, Katherine. "Behind America's Decline in Math, Science, and Technology." U.S. News & World Report, November 13, 2013. Accessed April 15, 2018. usnews.com/news/articles/2013/11/13/behind-americas-decline-in-math-science-and-technology.

Clifford, Catherine. "Elon Musk teases flying cars: 'Rocket tech applied to a car opens up revolutionary possibilities.'" CNBC.com. November 20, 2017, cnbc.com/2017/11/20/elon-musk-teases-flying-tesla-roadsters.html.

Desilver, Drew. "Growth from Asia drives surge in U.S. foreign students." Pew Research Center/National Center for Education Statistics. June 18, 2015. pewresearch.org/fact-tank/2015/06/18/growth-from-asia-drives-surge-in-u-s-foreign-students.

"Fast-Forwarding to a Future of On-Demand Urban Air Transportation." Uber.com. October/November 2016. uber.com/elevate.pdf.

Galeon, Dom and Kristin Houser. "Google Glass Is Back, and It's No Longer Meant for Everyone." July 18, 2017. futurism.com/google-glass-is-back-and-its-no-longer-meant-for-everyone.

Gallup. "More K-12 Computer Science Classes Teach Programming/Coding." Gallup.com. October 20, 2016. news.gallup.com/poll/196511/computer-science-classes-teach-programming-coding.aspx.

Hagan, Jean. "Realizing 2030: Dell Technologies Research Explores the Next Era of Human-Machine Partnerships." Institute for the Future website. July 12, 2017. iftf.org/future-now/article-detail/realizing-2030-dell-technologies-research-explores-the-next-era-of-human-machine-partnerships.

Krasley, Sara. "The 6 Questions That Lead to New Innovations." *Fast Company*. February 3, 2012. fastcompany.com/1679231/the-6-questions-that-lead-to-new-innovations.

Malik, Tariq. "SpaceX's Jaw-Dropping Rocket Launch Wows Spectators Across Southern California." Space.com. December 23, 2017. space.com/39197-spacex-spectacular-rocket-launch-views.html.

Musk, Elon. "Tesla and SpaceX: Elon Musk's Industrial Empire." By Scott Pelley. CBS News. March 30, 2014. cbsnews.com/news/tesla-and-spacex-elon-musks-industrial-empire.

"Public School Teacher Salaries." Salary.com. Accessed April 15, 2018. www1.salary.com/Public-School-Teacher-Salary.html.

Sandford, Stephen and Jay Heinrichs. *The Gravity Well: America's Next, Greatest Mission*. Pacific Grove, CA: Gavia Books, 2016.

"STEM Depiction Opportunities." WhiteHouse.gov. Accessed April 15, 2018. obamawhitehouse.archives.gov/sites/default/files/microsites/ostp/imageofstemdepictiondoc_02102016_clean.pdf.

Umoh, Ruth. "The US has a shortage of tech workers. Here's how kids and schools can solve the problem." CNBC.com. August 23, 2017. cnbc.com/2017/08/23/why-we-have-a-shortage-of-tech-workers-in-the-u-s.html.

Wackler, Ted, Evan Cooke, and Terah Lyons. "Harnessing the Potential of Unmanned Aircraft Systems Technology." August 2, 2016. obamawhitehouse.archives.gov/blog/2016/08/02/harnessing-potential-unmanned-aircraft-systems-technology.

100Kin10. "10 Big Insights on Teaching, Learning, and STEM Education: 100Kin10's Trends Report for 2017." 100Kin10.org. Retrieved January 29, 2018. 100kin10.org/news/10-big-insights-on-teaching-learning-and-stem-education-100kin10-s-trends-report-for-2017.

# MORE BOOKS FROM EDTECHTEAM PRESS

## edtechteam.com/books

### THE HYPERDOC HANDBOOK
#### Digital Lesson Design Using Google Apps
By Lisa Highfill, Kelly Hilton, and Sarah Landis

The HyperDoc Handbook is a practical reference guide for all K–12 educators who want to transform their teaching into blended-learning environments. The HyperDoc Handbook is a bestselling book that strikes the perfect balance between pedagogy and how-to tips while also providing ready-to-use lesson plans to get you started with HyperDocs right away.

### INNOVATE WITH IPAD
#### Lessons to Transform Learning
By Karen Lirenman and Kristen Wideen

Written by two primary teachers, this book provides a complete selection of clearly explained, engaging, open-ended lessons to change the way you use iPad with students at home or in the classroom. It features downloadable task cards, student-created examples, and extension ideas to use with your students. Whether you have access to one iPad for your entire class or one for each student, these lessons will help you transform learning in your classroom.

## THE SPACE
### A Guide for Educators
#### By Rebecca Louise Hare and Robert Dillon

*The Space* supports the conversation around revolution happening in education today concerning the reshaping of school spaces. This book goes well beyond the ideas for learning-space design that focuses on Pinterest-perfect classrooms and instead discusses real and practical ways to design learning spaces that support and drive learning.

## CLASSROOM MANAGEMENT IN THE DIGITAL AGE
### Effective Practices for Technology-Rich Learning Spaces
#### By Patrick Green and Heather Dowd

*Classroom Management in the Digital Age* helps guide and support teachers through the new landscape of device-rich classrooms. It provides practical strategies to novice and expert educators alike who want to maximize learning and minimize distraction. Learn how to keep up with the times while limiting time wasters and senseless screen-staring time.

## THE GOOGLE APPS GUIDEBOOK
### Lessons, Activities, and Projects Created by Students for Teachers
#### By Kern Kelley and the Tech Sherpas

*The Google Apps Guidebook* is filled with great ideas for the classroom from the voice of the students themselves. Each chapter introduces an engaging project that teaches students (and teachers) how to use one of Google's powerful tools. Projects are differentiated for a variety of age ranges and can be adapted for most content areas.

## CODE IN EVERY CLASS
### How All Educators Can Teach Programming
By Kevin Brookhouser and Ria Megnin

In *Code in Every Class,* Kevin Brookhouser and Ria Megnin explain why computer science is critical to your students' future success. With lesson ideas and step-by-step instruction, they show you how to take tech education into your own hands and open a world of opportunities to your students. And here's the best news: You *don't* have to be a computer genius to teach the basics of coding.

## MAKING YOUR SCHOOL SOMETHING SPECIAL
### Enhance Learning, Build Confidence, and Foster Success at Every Level
By Rushton Hurley

In *Making Your School Something Special,* educator and international speaker Rushton Hurley explores the mindsets, activities, and technology that make for great learning. You'll learn how to create strong learning activities and make your school a place where students and teachers alike want to be—because it's where they feel energized, inspired, and *special.*

## MAKING YOUR TEACHING SOMETHING SPECIAL
### 50 Simple Ways to Become a Better Teacher
By Rushton Hurley

In the second book in his series, Rushton Hurley highlights key areas of teaching that play a part in shaping your success as an educator. Whether you are finding your way as a brand new teacher or are a seasoned teacher who is looking for some powerful ideas, this book offers inspiration and practical advice to help you make this year your best yet.

## THE GOOGLE CARDBOARD BOOK
### Explore, Engage, and Educate with Virtual Reality
An EdTechTeam Collaboration

In *The Google Cardboard Book,* EdTechTeam trainers and leaders offer step-by-step instructions on how to use virtual reality technology in your classroom—no matter what subject you teach. You'll learn what tools you need (and how affordable they can be), which apps to start with, and how to view, capture, and share 360° videos and images.

## TRANSFORMING LIBRARIES
### A Toolkit for Innovators, Makers, and Seekers
By Ron Starker

In the Digital Age, it's more important than ever for libraries to evolve into gathering points for collaboration, spaces for innovation, and places where authentic learning occurs. In *Transforming Libraries,* Ron Starker reveals ways to make libraries makerspaces, innovation centers, community commons, and learning design studios that engage multiple forms of intelligence.

## INTENTION
### Critical Creativity in the Classroom
By Amy Burvall and Dan Ryder

Inspiring and exploring creativity opens pathways for students to use creative expression to demonstrate content knowledge, critical thinking, and the problem solving that will serve them best no matter what their futures may bring. *Intention* offers a collection of ideas, activities, and reasons for bringing creativity to every lesson.

## The Conference Companion
### Sketchnotes, Doodles, and Creative Play for Teaching and Learning
By Becky Green

Wherever you are learning, whatever your doodle comfort level, this jovial notebook is your buddy. Sketchnotes, doodles, and creative play await both you and your students. Part workshop, part journal, and part sketchbook, these simple and light-hearted scaffolds and lessons will transform your listening and learning experiences while providing creative inspiration for your classroom.

## Bring the World to Your Classroom
### Using Google Geo Tools
By Kelly Kermode and Kim Randall

We live and work in a global society, but many students have only a very small community or neighborhood as their frame of reference. Expand their horizons and help them increase their understanding of how they fit in the global landscape using Google Geo Tools. This book is packed full of how-tos and sample projects to get you and your learners moving forward with mapping, exploring, and making connections to the world around you.

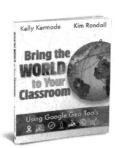

## 50 Ways to Use YouTube in the Classroom
By Patrick Green

Your students are already accessing YouTube, so why not meet them where they are as consumers of information? By using the tools they choose, you can maximize their understanding in ways that matter. *50 Ways to Use YouTube in the Classroom* is an accessible guide that will improve your teaching, your students' learning, and your classroom culture.

## ILLUMINATE
### Technology Enhanced Learning
By Bethany Petty

In *Illuminate*, author, educator, and technology trainer Bethany Petty explains how to use technology to improve your students' learning experiences. You'll learn specific how-tos for using a wide variety of apps and tools as well as the why behind using technology. Meet your students' needs and make learning memorable using technology enhanced learning.

## MORE NOW
### A Message from the Future for the Educators of Today
By Mark Wagner

The priorities and processes of education must change if we are going to prepare students for their future. In *More Now*, EdTechTeam Founder Mark Wagner, explores the six essential elements of effective school change: courageous leaders, empowered teachers, student agency, inspiring spaces, robust infrastructure, and engaged communities. You'll learn from educational leaders, teachers, and technologists how you can make each of these essential elements part of your school or district culture—starting now.

## 40 Ways to Inject Creativity into Your Classroom with Adobe Spark

By Ben Forta and Monica Burns

Experienced educators Ben Forta and Monica Burns offer step-by-step guidance on how to incorporate this powerful tool into your classroom in ways that are meaningful and relevant. They present **40 fun and practical lesson plans** suitable for a variety of ages and subjects as well as 15 graphic organizers to get you started. With the tips, suggestions, and encouragement in this book, you'll find everything you need to inject creativity into *your* classroom using Adobe Spark.

## The Top 50 Chrome Extensions for the Classroom

By Christopher Craft, PhD

If you've ever wished there were a way to add more minutes to the day, Chrome Extensions just may be the answer. In *The Top 50 Chrome Extensions for the Classroom,* you'll learn time-saving tips and efficiency tricks that will help reduce the amount of time spent in lesson preparation and administrative tasks—so you can spend more time with students.

# ABOUT THE AUTHORS

**Rachael Mann** is a speaker, author, and founder of #TeachLikeTED, an organization that provides teachers, students, and leaders with tools for presentation literacy.

Rachael uses her voice and her expertise to broaden the conversation around education reform, and to amplify the voices of teachers and students. Prior to #TeachLikeTED, Rachael was the Network to Transform Teaching and STEM professional learning director for Northern Arizona University and state director for Educators Rising Arizona, and she currently provides professional development for West-MEC.

A former high school career and technical education teacher, and hailing from a family of educators, she has fourteen years of classroom teaching experience. She serves on the ACTE Region V Policy Committee, the NCLA executive board, and the ACTEAZ executive board. She is a founding member of the Council on the Future of Education. Rachael is a Google Certified Educator with a master's degree in educational leadership from Northern Arizona University. She currently lives in Phoenix, Arizona, and enjoys hiking, tennis, and good eats.

**Stephen P. Sandford** is currently systems engineering director at Stinger, Ghaffarian Technologies, Inc. He uses his NASA experience on a wide variety of assignments from engineering future satellite repair and asteroid utilization technologies to new business development, corporate strategy, and Space policy formulation.

Prior to his current position, Stephen was director for Space technology and exploration at NASA's Langley Research Center, Hampton, Virginia. There he led teams of engineers, researchers, and mission architects focused on the toughest human exploration challenges, creating high payoff, cross-cutting Space technologies. He was responsible for the Center's program implementation of Space and technology programs, as well as planning and advocating for the best utilization of the broad suite of Center aerospace expertise and facilities.

Stephen Sandford's twenty-eight-year career in aerospace with NASA spanned electro-optical engineering and research, systems engineering, line and project management, and senior leadership positions at Langley Research Center with long-term assignments at Johnson Space Center and Headquarters. He has worked closely with teams from every NASA Center over his career as part of his contribution to the development of Space-based electro-optical remote sensing systems and flight test vehicles enabling Earth science research, novel space technologies, and planetary and human exploration. As Langley's engineering director from 2004 to 2012, he led the organization's engineering contributions to many successful flight projects for Shuttle return-to-flight, for Earth science satellites, and for experimental vehicles for next generation human spaceflight. This includes the successful flight tests of inflatable reentry systems, the Ares 1-X vehicle, and the Pad Abort test for the Orion Launch Abort System.

Sandford has received numerous awards, including two NASA honor award medals and several group achievement awards. He joined the federal senior executive service in 2001. He is a member of Phi Beta Kappa.

Stephen Sandford received his BS in physics from Randolph Macon, MS in electrical engineering at the University of Virginia, and his MS in optical science from the University of Arizona. He currently lives in York County, Virginia. He enjoys reading, backpacking, volleyball, cycling, and running.

Made in the USA
Columbia, SC
19 June 2019